Consistently Pro-Life

Consistently Pro-Life

The Ethics of Bloodshed in Ancient Christianity

Rob Arner

with a foreword by J. Jayakiran Sebastian

To Carol:

Pax Christi!

— Rob Arner

PICKWICK *Publications* · Eugene, Oregon

CONSISTENTLY PRO-LIFE
The Ethics of Bloodshed in Ancient Christianity

Pickwick Publications
An Imprint of Wipf and Stock Publishers
199 W. 8th Ave., Suite 3
Eugene, OR 97401

www.wipfandstock.com

ISBN 13: 978-1-60608-612-4

Cataloging-in-Publication data:

Arner, Rob.

   Consistently pro-life : the ethics of bloodshed in ancient Christianity / Rob Arner ; foreword by J. Jayakiran Sebastian.

   xvi + 136 p. ; 23 cm. Includes bibliographical references.

   ISBN 13: 978-1-60608-612-4

   1. War — Religious aspects — Christianity. 2. Abortion — Religious aspects —Christianity — History. I. Sebastian, J. Jayakiran, 1958– . II. Title.

BT736.2 .A75 2010

Manufactured in the U.S.A.

Contents

Contents

Foreword

Rob Arner's detailed and comprehensive study on ancient Christian perspectives on war, peace, and violence in pre-Constantinian Christianity deserves commendation on several counts. It offers a careful reading of a very wide range of texts taken not as snippets from here and there, but from within the varied contexts in which they were written. In addition, it places these texts from the early teachers of faith in a neat sequence that has the merit of enabling the readers to trace the growth of the Christian church within the Roman empire and understand how the leaders of this movement sought to come to terms with the reality of violence not only in everyday life but as part of a brutal system of imposing discipline in the wide-ranging territories and on the variety of peoples that had come under the orbit of Rome. The work also analyzes these writings in terms of clarifying the underlying scriptural ideas, which involved not only a rereading and reinterpretation of texts from the Hebrew scriptures, but also the valorization of the teachings of Jesus and his early interpreters, including Paul. These teaching offered a counter-cultural model that provided the readers of these writings and the adherents of the new religious movement which was in the process of coalescing into a recognizable entity, a way of being and a way of believing, however impractical and illogical it may have seemed, over against the prevailing taken-for-granted ideology of the dominant power of that time. To affirm that life in all its complexity and all its fullness was precious, and that in a society that was deeply stratified and organized into more or less rigid and static hierarchies all human beings were worthy of recognition as God's children was indeed a revolutionary teaching, which led to incredulity, disparagement, and open hostility, not to say anything of being considered subversive and against the established principles of the state.

The period in which the Christian church emerged was characterized by war and violence as well as the concerted effort on the part of the ruling authorities to mercilessly impose what they considered conditions conducive to peace on the far-flung territories of the empire. Paradoxically, civilization and cruelty went hand-in-hand. The Roman amphitheatre, not only in the capital, but also in other cities and towns of the empire, with its games designed to entertain the citizens with spectacular shows were organized in such a way so as to embody both entertainment and edification, as well as showcase the ability of the sponsors to offer exotic demonstrations of power. Most of these comprised of exquisitely cruel activities, like the gladiator shows, combat between men, sometimes professionals, and often criminals, using a variety of weapons; combat between men and animals, and between a range and variety of beasts. This, apart from the chariot races and athletic contests, formed the staple of the entertainment industry.

Roman laws too were framed to discipline and punish, and were implemented with ruthless determination. Probably the most noteworthy of the public punishments was crucifixion, which was designed to impose the maximum of pain for a prolonged period, and admonish the spectators and passers-by through a lingering demonstration of vicious cruelty. Those condemned to die on the cross were often flogged with whips, in which pieces of bone and metal had been embedded, and although weakened by the loss of blood and battered by humiliation, were often forced to walk naked to the place of execution, bearing the cross-beam on which they were to hang and die. The bodies were often just left there, to serve as food for the carrion birds and the foraging dogs at the foot of the crosses, and to function as a stark reminder that under the benevolence of the peace of Rome, lay the unquestioned authority of those who held the power of life and death, and who had no compunction in imposing the harshest penalties of the law on those who did not conform to the duties and obligations expected of the inhabitants of the scattered and often restless domains.

Rob Arner forces us to confront a world that is seemingly far from where we are today, a world distant even to those who profess allegiance to the teachings of the man from Nazareth. The coming together of church and empire after the so-called "conversion" of the Roman emperor Constantine in the early fourth century CE has had enormous consequences for the ongoing life of the church. A movement born in and through adversity, quickly took the lead in becoming the aggressor; a movement that claimed to reach out to the least and the lost, easily took on the role of patron and provider; a movement that asserted the primacy of the local congregations and the varieties of the gifts of ministry, rapidly became centralized, institutionalized, and strongly hierarchical; a movement that sought to canalize difference and diversity into vibrancy and variety, quickly sought to impose uniformity through standardization of doctrine and practice. The fact that these attempts did not succeed is another story. Nevertheless what is important is that in the early centuries faced with confrontation and clashes, challenges and controversies, competition and conflict, the recovery of courage and conviction, calmness and composure, commitment and confidence are lessons well worth recollecting as one reads through this important book.

Robin Lane Fox, in concluding his fine book on the legacy of Greece and Rome, reflects on the Roman emperor Hadrian, who ruled from the turn of the first century CE into the first two decades of the second, and notes that "he had no idea that the Christians, whose harassment he regulated, would then overturn this world by antiquity's greatest realignment of freedom and justice. . . ." (Robin Lane Fox, *The Classical World: An Epic History of Greece and Rome* [London: Penguin, 2006] 606). Rob Arner has done us a great service by placing before us the sources and resources that enabled this fledging movement to consistently affirm the sacredness of life, and thus turn the world upside down and harness those forces which could make the world a better place to live in, lessons that to a large extent that have been ignored, but lessons that we can return to with profit in a world where violence seems to be in the ascendancy, a world where we have to consistently and constantly reaffirm and realign the power of peace.

Rev. Dr. J. Jayakiran Sebastian
H. George Anderson Professor of Mission and Cultures
Director, Multicultural Mission Resource Center
The Lutheran Theological Seminary at Philadelphia

Preface

"WHO WOULD JESUS KILL?"

This was the title of the PowerPoint presentation given to my college Christian fellowship group that started me down the path of exploring an ethic of consistent, Christocentric nonviolence that will be the subject of this book. I had been raised in the United Methodist Church, and before that point in my life, had never given a second thought to the relationship between Christianity and violence. Because of my upbringing in a church that honored and celebrated the courage of American military veterans and those who made the "ultimate sacrifice,"[1] and which raised few moral scruples at the issue of abortion of an unwanted child, I had largely taken for granted what I had been acculturated to believe—that killing can be reconciled with Christian discipleship, with the moral paradigm of the cross, and with the command to love your enemies.

These uncritical assumptions were severely shaken following that presentation and discussion, in which we walked through the gospel texts with an honest and open ear to hearing what they might have to say concerning Christianity and violence, or the compatibility of the coercive sword with the kenotic cross. Feeling so called in that direction of exploration, when I received the call to go to seminary, I chose a seminary affiliated with the historic peace churches in order to dive deeper into this perspective on the gospel which strangely attracted me. During my seminary studies, I began to hear about the ancient Christian church—which, I was told, refused to kill or cooperate with violence in any form—

---

1. For an excellent deconstruction of the misappropriation of "sacrifice" rhetoric by the military culture, see Stanley Hauerwas, "Sacrificing the Sacrifices of War." Hauerwas argues that the destructive effects of taking a human life—not only on the one killed but on the killer as well—can only be healed through the cross of Christ and the work of the church, whose alternative to war is and has always been worship. In light of the resurrection, "The sacrifices of war are no longer necessary. We are now free to live free of the necessity of violence and killing. War and the sacrifices of war have come to an end. War has been abolished" (95).

a fact which deeply resonated with my growing understanding of what it meant to follow Jesus. This project is an effort at recovery of that ancient Christian ethic, and an assertion of its relevance for the tasks facing the church today. Specifically, it is a repudiation of piecemeal or *ad hoc* approaches to Christian ethics through the realization of the interconnectedness of disparate issues involving the killing of human persons.

As I see it, there are two major problems with the way moral issues are deliberated and acted upon in modern Christian (and especially Protestant) circles. First, a strange phenomenon has occurred in which Christians have generally subordinated or ceased asking entirely the vital questions "Which course of action is most consistent with my identity as a disciple of Jesus Christ?" and "What does God require of me?" These questions have been replaced with "What is the most effective way to achieve the ends I desire?" Or, put less cynically, "How can we most efficiently transform the world for God?" In other words, many modern Christians have tended to prioritize *effectiveness* over *faithfulness*.[2] The question of the appropriateness of the means is subordinated as long as the desired ends (even good ends, like greater social justice, or the protection of human life) are achieved.[3] This is deeply problematic from a New Testament

---

2. John Howard Yoder helpfully observes that "when Christians count among their number a monarch, or the majority in a democratic system, or a sizable and significant minority in a pluralistic democratic system, it can be practically taken for granted that one way, perhaps the only right way to do moral deliberation is to work out a consequentialist calculation of the direction one wants the whole system to take" (*Priestly Kingdom*, 96). Yoder regards the temptation to "make history turn out right," no matter how well-intentioned, as one of the most fundamental mistakes Christians can make in moral discernment, because of the temptation to utilize evil means in order to achieve a greater good.

3. Martin Luther King Jr. paraphrases the common argument thusly: "So, if you're seeking to develop a just society, they say, the important thing is to get there, and the means are really unimportant; any means will do so long as they get you there—they may be violent, they may be untruthful means; they may even be unjust means to a just end. There have been those who have argued that throughout history. But we will never have peace in the world until men everywhere recognize that ends are not cut off from means, because the means represent the idea in the making, and the end in process, and ultimately you can't reach good ends through evil means, because the means represent the seed and the end represents the tree." And, leveling criticism at all ideologies that would say that we must kill in the name of peace or make war in order that peace might prevail, King concludes that "one day we must come to see that peace is not merely a distant goal we seek, but that it is a means by which we arrive at that goal. We must pursue peaceful ends through peaceful means. All of this is saying that, in the final analysis, means and

point of view, which views the means as just as important, if not *more* important, than the ends.[4] Thus, a modern articulation of Christian ethics should recover faithfulness to Jesus as of the utmost importance. Fidelity to Christ must preempt consequentialist calculations of cause and effect, or means and ends.

Secondly, many recently articulated approaches to ethics have been (from my perspective at least) sloppy, *ad hoc*, and piecemeal at best. The modern trend has been to compartmentalize and isolate individual ethical issues from one another, as if what we say in matters of sexual ethics (for example) had no bearing on ethical economic stewardship. Or, to take the cases of what I'll be arguing, there is a tendency to treat killing in war and abortion as entirely unrelated issues.[5] In this book I will explore some of

---

ends must cohere because the end is preexistent in the means, and ultimately destructive means cannot bring about constructive ends" ("Christmas Sermon on Peace," 255).

4. The book of Revelation in particular is filled with summons to act in ways that seem bafflingly ineffective by normal human standards. Revelation 13:10 and 14:12 for example call upon the people of God to patiently and faithfully endure sufferings and persecutions without retaliation, waiting on God's sure vindication rather than trying to vindicate themselves through retaliatory violence.

5. Nat Hentoff, a self-described "Jewish atheist," came to realize the interconnectedness of these "life issues" along the way to embracing a consistently pro-life stance. He recalls a speech he made before the (mostly Christian) members of a Right to Life convention in which he pointed out that "pro-lifers . . . ought to be opposing capital punishment and nuclear armament and the Reagan budget with its dedicated care for missiles, as it cuts funds for Woman/Infant/Children program that provides diet supplements and medical checkups for mothers in poverty. Surely, I said, they should not emulate the President . . . in being pro-life only up to the moment of birth. Well the faces before me began to close, and from the middle and back of the dining room there were shouts. I couldn't make out the words, but they were not approving. As I went on, there were more shouts as well as growls and table-thumping of an insistence that indicated a tumbrel awaited outside. I finally ended my speech to a chorus of howls, and several of the diners rushed toward the dais. I did not remember ever intending to die for this cause, but as it turned out the attacks were all verbal. Most of the disappointed listeners, once they caught their breath, charitably ascribed my failure to understand the total unrelatedness of nuclear arms and abortion to my not yet having found God" ("Indivisibility of Life and the Slippery Slope," 31). This attitude, sadly, has been far too typical of many in the anti-abortion movement in particular. Having been labeled "single-issue voters" by the mainstream media and the dominant modes of narrative discourse in the United States, many pro-lifers have taken this attitude to heart in their single-minded push against the violence of abortion. Typical of this failure to draw moral linkage is Curt Young's volume *The Least of These* in which he takes great pains (37–38) to distance the killing of *innocent* life (which he sees as forbidden by Exod 10:13) from the execution of criminals or lethal self-defense (which he believes is not). Likewise the linkage between the various issues of violence has proven equally elusive for those who murder abortionists in the name of protecting innocent fetal life.

these fundamental, underlying assumptions, and make the case for a link between all the "life issues" (e.g., abortion, war, capital punishment, euthanasia, economic justice, and compassion for the neighbor) that, while not collapsing them into a single issue, nevertheless holds them together, so that for example, our attitudes on how we treat the "least of these" in our midst directly affects the way we regard the unborn child, the victims of war, or even the armed, hostile enemy. This linkage is both theological and anthropological, as all members of God's creation are members in one interactive global community, and the welfare of one impacts the welfare of us all. To me, this linkage is an imperative, as God pours his love on the just and the unjust alike, and Jesus, who is no respecter of persons, calls us to do the same.

My experience of articulating a consistent ethic of life among different kinds of Christians meets with similar responses from those who fail to see this vital linkage. When I speak in "conservative"[6] Christian circles about the importance of opposing abortion on demand because of the tragedy of human lives lost in the over 1.2 *million* abortions performed annually in the United States,[7] heads nod appreciatively and shouts of "Amen!" echo through the halls. But when I speak in those same circles about ending the military occupation of Iraq or why the violence of soldiers is so incompatible with the life of Christian discipleship, tongues wag, Romans 13:1–7 is cited out of context, and complaints arise about my failure to "support the troops." Likewise, when I speak in "liberal" Christian circles about the millions killed as a result of American wars and

---

6. Here, I must regrettably use the standard, yet deeply problematic liberal/conservative dichotomy to narrate my experiences in this paragraph. While recognizing the fluidity of these categories, and the fact that few, if any people fit neatly into "conservative" and "liberal" Christian stereotypes with any real regularity, I have found that these two overly-broad generalizations actually do significantly describe two major constituencies of American Christians, both of whom are largely ignorant of, or outright deny, the connection between major "life issues." Sociologist Edith Bogue has found in her research that among the American public, there is "a division between respect-for-life issues in the domains of private morality and personal behavior (passive euthanasia, suicide, physical and social reasons for abortion) and those that involve social policies (capital punishment, military spending, welfare spending, and environmental spending" ["Does the Seamless Garment Fit?" 81]). Those I term "conservatives" usually speak out on pro-life issues in private morality, while "liberals" are more concerned with pro-life issues in social policies.

7. This estimate has been independently confirmed by both the Centers for Disease Control and the Alan Guttmacher Institute, the research arm of Planned Parenthood. See for example http://www.guttmacher.org/pubs/journals/4000608.pdf

policies of imperialism and the responsibility of Christians to speak out against these injustices, I am greeted with an enthusiastic reception and polite applause. But when I challenge those same "liberal" Christians over their uncritical approval of the violence of abortion and acceptance of the unbiblical cultural framing of the issue that pits the "rights" of the mother against the "rights" of her unborn child, I get stony silence, murmurs of dissent, and uncomfortable shifting in chairs. The consistent ethic of life of the gospel of Jesus is, I contend, neither "liberal" nor "conservative," for it cuts across all human ideological distinctions, challenging all to uphold the dignity and value of each human person from conception to death.

This is a book about killing. Specifically, when and under what circumstances is it morally justifiable to take human life? Even more specifically, what moral demands might the gospel of Jesus Christ make upon those whom Christ has called to take up the cross and follow him, with respect to the taking of human life? In this slim volume, addressed specifically to my fellow Christians, I seek to problematize heretofore unexamined assumptions about the intentional destruction of human beings. Both "liberals" and "conservatives" will find themselves challenged by the witness of the ancient Christian church, which we will see consistently opposed the destruction and degradation of human persons in any form.

This is a work in two parts, one an effort at cultural criticism of the contemporary American, and specifically Christian, ethos, the other a historiographic presentation of the moral convictions of the ancient Christians with respect to questions of killing. Part One takes its point of departure from the murder of Dr. George Tiller by a man who ostensibly hated Tiller's profession—for Tiller was an abortion doctor. In this part, I analyze three "moments" in the cycle of violence of which abortion is a part—the actual violence of abortion, the violence advocated and used by a few on the extremist fringe of the antiabortion movement, and the state-sanctioned violence that is used retributively against the abortionist's murderer. What would it mean, I ask, to be consistently pro-life in a way that cares not just for fetuses or unborn children, but also about their mothers, their fathers, and every member of human society? Then in Part Two, I offer the witness of the ancient Christian church as an example of how we modern Christians might consistently apply the gospel precepts toward questions of the taking of human life. Though a new taxonomy that categorizes the patristic witness according to individual issues such as abortion/infanticide, killing in war, and the bloody Roman "games,"

I hope to demonstrate that the early church consistently opposed the killing of human persons, and to suggest that the discipline and moral clarity of the ancient Christians (on issues of violence, at least) can show us a new way forward in a time of polarizing culture wars.

As with any author's efforts, this work would not have been possible without a number of individuals to whom I wish to express my deep gratitude. First, thanks to the patristics professor at the Lutheran Theological Seminary at Philadelphia, J. Jayakiran Sebastian under whose auspices I had originally written the historical research component of this work. Dr. Sebastian has also graciously contributed the foreword that appears in this volume. Second, I am grateful to the community of Eastern Mennonite Seminary in Harrisonburg, Virginia—an amazing community of faith and service that nurtured me spiritually and provided me with the intellectual training I needed at just the right time in my life. Third, I wish to thank my students from a course I taught at LTSP called "The Cross and the Sword: Theological Ethics of Violence," who not only provided me with valuable feedback on an early draft of this work, but allowed me the space to try out new ideas and teaching techniques that allowed this work to come to fruition.

Finally, I dedicate this work to my infinitely patient and compassionate wife Lori, and to Grace Emily Arner, our daughter whom we hope to meet for the first time on her birthday in roughly two months. I pray to the Prince of Peace that she may grow up in a world without violence.

Philadelphia, August 11, 2009

PART ONE

Consistently Pro-Life?

1

Tragedy at Pentecost

MURDER IN WICHITA

THE HOLY SPIRIT CERTAINLY never willed *this*.

~

On Pentecost Sunday, inside Reformation Lutheran Church of Wichita, Kansas, the ushers and greeters are busy preparing for the morning's worship service. As on any other Sunday, there are hands to be shaken, church bulletins to be organized and handed out, visitors to be welcomed. But this is to be no ordinary Sunday.

Pentecost is the day that Christians commemorate the beginning of the church, the day when the Holy Spirit came upon the believers in power, as narrated in the second chapter of the Acts of the Apostles. The sound of a roaring wind, tongues of fire, and the newfound ability to speak in many languages were among the signs and wonders that accompanied the pouring out of the Spirit, testifying to the church's commission to spread the good news of what God had done through Jesus among the nations.

As the worship service begins in Wichita, one of the ushers, a bespectacled, grandfatherly-looking figure named George, takes up his place at the entrance, prepared to hand bulletins to any late-comers who might arrive. George is approached by a lone, middle-aged man who had been attending services at Reformation Lutheran for the past several weeks. As George smiles and prepares to offer the man the church bulletin, the visitor reaches down and draws a pistol. He calmly aims it at the startled George, and fires. George is killed instantly by a single bullet to the head. He collapses, scattering church bulletins everywhere. George's assailant then turns and flees the scene, threatening two would-be heroes with the gun as he gets into his car and speeds off.

～

As shocking as this murder scene in a house of worship on Pentecost is, what separates this particular homicide from the over 10,000 murders that occur every year in the United States alone? It was not the setting or the timing, but the victim and the motive. "George" is Dr. George Tiller, the notorious or courageous (depending on your perspective) abortionist, famous for being one of the very few abortion providers in the country willing to offer that service as late as the end of the third trimester of pregnancy.

Known by many supporters and opponents as the "doctor of last resort"[1] because of his willingness to perform abortions in some of the most extreme cases turned down by most other physicians, Tiller was a lightning rod of controversy. Frequently outspoken in his support for what he felt to be his life's calling, Tiller had by his own admission performed over 60,000 abortions in his thirty-year career. In an indication of the controversy his profession continues to stir up among Christian churches, Tiller had been excommunicated by his previous church, a congregation of the strongly anti-abortion Lutheran Church-Missouri Synod, for refusing to cease his practice.[2] Reformation Lutheran Church, which had embraced Dr. Tiller and his profession, is a congregation of the Evangelical Lutheran Church in America. The fact that such a polarizing figure could be excommunicated by one Christian group because of their belief that his occupation was incompatible with the life of Christian discipleship, while being welcomed with open arms by another Christian group with the same theological heritage is itself a sorry commentary on the schizophrenic nature of the modern American Christian church, pointing to deep discrepancies in theological and moral foundations in the church's various expressions. Combating a similar sort of moral schizophrenia is the subject this book.

---

1. Warner, "Dr. Tiller's Important Job."

2. According to Uwe Siemon-Netto of the LCMS's Concordia Seminary, in an blog posting from 2008, "Remembering Collective Shame."

THE "SPIN" BEGINS

The reaction to George Tiller's murder has been strong. Pro-abortion groups began the process of Tiller's hagiography just as quickly as anti-abortion groups had demonized him. The website of the National Abortion Federation, for example, contains a star-spangled banner alongside Tiller's portrait, bearing the inscription "Remembering an American Hero—Dr. George Tiller."[3] Likewise, Tiller's colleague at his Wichita abortion clinic, Dr. LeRoy Carhart, speaking at a memorial service for his fallen friend, told the assembled mourners that Tiller's assassination was "the equivalent of Martin Luther King being assassinated." He continued: "This is the equivalent of Pearl Harbor, the sinking of the Lusitania and any other major historic event where we've tolerated the intolerable for too long."[4] The president of the Religious Coalition for Reproductive Choice, which boasted Dr. Tiller as a member, called him a "humble, courageous man who dedicated his life to justice, liberty and freedom" and "a true American hero."[5] Tiller has even been called "a religious martyr in the fullest classical sense," killed because he acted in accord with his conscience, religious convictions, and moral choices.[6]

Even as the accolades by Tiller's supporters and friends were pouring in, his many fierce critics and opponents were also expressing themselves. Troy Newman, current president of the anti-abortion activist group Operation Rescue which had in recent years relocated its national headquarters to Wichita in order to directly oppose Dr. Tiller's practice, was filled with mixed emotions. In an interview with the *New York Times* (before it was announced that Tiller's clinic would be closing permanently), Newman expressed his shock and fear that the murder would encourage similar violence around the country. Referring to Tiller's alleged assailant, he lamented, "This idiot did more to damage the pro-life movement

3. http://www.prochoice.org/tillerblog/ (accessed June 15, 2009).

4. Duin, "Doctor Likens Tiller's Killing to MLK's." Interestingly, the following day, members of the late Dr. King's family responded negatively to Dr. Carhart's comparison. Alveda King, the niece of the slain civil rights leader, was indignant. "For LeRoy Carhart to mention the murder of Dr. Martin Luther King Jr., who worked through peaceful and nonviolent means, in the same breath with that of George Tiller, whose work ended peace and brought violence to babies in the womb, is offensive beyond belief," she said in an interview, "The analogy is just wrong." See Duin, "MLK Kin Decries Comparison to Tiller."

5. Statement of Reverend Carlton W. Veazey, on behalf of the RCRC (June 1, 2009).

6. Waskow, "Murder is Murder and Abortion is Not."

than you can imagine."[7] After Tiller's family announced that the clinic would not reopen after the doctor's assassination, Newman expressed his gratitude that the goal for which he and his organization had labored had finally been accomplished, but deplored the way it came about. "We are thankful that Tiller's clinic will not reopen and thankful that Wichita is now abortion-free," he said, but emphasized that "this is a bittersweet moment for us at Operation Rescue. We have worked very hard for this day, but we wish it would have come through the peaceful, legal channels that we were pursuing."[8]

Some anti-abortion advocates were less regretful of Tiller's murder. Randall Terry, the original high-profile founder of Operation Rescue, did not equivocate in his opinion of Tiller. While denouncing the "vigilante justice" of the murderer, Terry called Tiller "one of the most evil men on the planet; every bit as vile as the Nazi war criminals who were hunted down, tried, and sentenced after they participated in the 'legal' murder of the Jews that fell into their hands."[9] Though he personally denounced the way in which Tiller was stopped, he told the National Press Club that Tiller was "a mass murderer" who "reaped what he sowed."[10]

These disparate reactions to the murder of such a polarizing figure rest on the interpretation of what Dr. Tiller did for a living. If, as his defenders claim, Tiller's occupation was one of therapy and healing for women faced with unintended pregnancy, then Tiller can rightly be called a hero for facing the daily harassment and protests outside his workplace.[11]

7. "Good God, do not close this abortion clinic for this reason," he said. "Every kook in the world will get some notion." Davey, "Closed Clinic Leaves Abortion Protesters at a Loss."

8. Statement on Operation Rescue's website dated June 9, 2009. Online: http://www.operationrescue.org/archives/tiller-clinic-will-permanently-close-while-ksbha-says-abortion-investigation-still-pending/ (accessed June 15, 2009).

9. "Dr. Tiller's Death: Randall Terry Releases Video for Pro-life Leaders Concerning Dr. Tiller's Killing" (May 31, 2009). Online: http://www.christiannewswire.com/news/7392310537.html (accessed June 16, 2009).

10. Rucker, "Pro-Life Activist Says Doctor 'Reaped What He Sowed.'"

11. His murder was not the first time he was physically attacked. In 1986, a pipe bomb caused over $100,000 in damage to his clinic (though no injuries were reported), and in 1993, Tiller was shot in both arms by a women who was waiting for him in the clinic's parking lot. In 1991, Tiller's Wichita clinic was the scene of the largest sustained anti-abortion demonstration in history during Operation Rescue's forty-five day "Summer of Mercy" campaign, that registered over 2,600 arrests of nonviolent clinic protesters. Through it all, he maintained a steely resolve to continue his work because of his conviction that it was indeed helping women.

But if, as his detractors assert, Tiller was guilty of deliberately taking thousands of human lives through legitimized, institutionalized murder, then the shock and horror of antiabortion advocates is justifiable.

THREE MOMENTS IN THE CYCLE OF VIOLENCE

As has been made clear in everything from domestic abuse to international wars, violence breeds more violence, and the slaying of Dr. Tiller, far from being an isolated case of killing, is itself part of a causal cycle of violence. It was preceded by human bloodshed, and additional human bloodshed may well follow it. This manifestation of the ubiquitous cycle of violence comprises three essential "moments" that can be isolated from one another:[12]

1. First, we have the killing of fetuses *in utero* via abortion. This was how Dr. Tiller made his living.

2. Second, Dr. Tiller is himself killed by an assassin in the shocking murder described above.

3. Third, Tiller's alleged murderer may, upon conviction, be killed himself by the state through the violence of capital punishment, as Paul Hill was executed for the 1994 murder of abortionist John Britton and his clinic escort James Barrett.

Nobody is *for* killing, of course. Reasonable people would assert their opposition in principle to killing a human being in most cases. Yet with few exceptions, most people will admit certain circumstances or instances in which they believe deliberate killing can be justified, if not in fact being a positive moral good. For each of the three moments in this violence cycle, there are those who would justify one of the three specific instances of killing, while denouncing the other two. In what follows, I will analyze examples of such justifications by those who would rationalize killing in one of those three specific moments in order to better understand what happens when we drop our moral scruples against violating the *imago Dei*

12. We should not forget, of course, to situate this cycle of violence amidst the events that precede and follow it. For example, abortions do not usually occur without cause and are often precipitated by tragic or extraordinary circumstances; they are sometimes themselves preceded by violent acts like rape. For our purposes here, however, we will be concentrating on the three moments of violence listed above, in order to understand how each of these three moments in the cycle are justified by those who practice and condone them.

in another human being and decide that we are justified in ending the life of our fellow human persons.

2

Justifications for the Violence of Abortion

IN THE FIRST INSTANCE, advocates of "abortion rights" justify feticide by appealing to classically liberal notions of freedom, privacy, and self-autonomy, as well as compassion for women in difficult situations. Many mainline Christian denominations have taken a similar position to the Evangelical Lutheran Church in America, which believes that "there can be sound reasons for ending a pregnancy through induced abortion,"[1] reasons which include when the physical life of the mother is at stake, when she has been raped, or when the child conceived is the product of an incestuous relationship. Typically, these so-called "hard cases" are at the center of abortion rights rhetoric, because they are the most clearly emotionally persuasive, tugging at the reader's empathetic heart-strings. A recent opinion piece in the *New York Times*, ruminating on "Dr. Tiller's Important Job" opens with a description of one of the most horrifically tragic circumstances of pregnancy imaginable—a nine-year-old girl who had conceived after being raped by her father. Had she carried the child to term, including natural labor and delivery, the article asserts, the experience "would have ripped her small body apart."[2]

These sorts of horror stories are at the forefront of pro-abortion arguments in modern America, attempting to put faces on some of the worst-case scenarios for which women undergo abortions. Yet these horrific circumstances do not represent the reality behind the post-*Roe v. Wade* world. These cases are used to justify more permissive laws and social attitudes toward abortions, attitudes which have led to well over *one million* abortions performed legally every year in the United States.

1. ELCA Social Statement on Abortion, approved August 1991. Online: http://archive.elca.org/socialstatements/abortion/.

2. Warner, "Dr. Tiller's Important Job."

The Alan Guttmacher Institute, a clearinghouse of abortion statistics and information, reported that in the year 2000, of the 1.2 million induced abortions performed in the United States, only 13,000 (only about 1%) were performed following cases of rape or incest, the "hard cases" most frequently cited in pro-abortion arguments.[3] If this is the case that the reality of most abortions are so radically different than the "hard cases" so often in the public eye in this debate, what are the reasons for the other 99% of abortions? According to the Guttmacher Institute,

> On average, women give at least three reasons for choosing abortion: three-fourths say that having a baby would interfere with work, school, or other responsibilities; about two-thirds say they cannot afford a child; and half say they do not want to be a single parent or are having problems with their husband or partner.[4]

No matter how or by whom the statistics are compiled, the vast majority of abortions performed in the United States have nothing to do with rape, incest, or threats to the mother's health, but occur rather as the result of perceived necessity ("I/we can't afford a baby right now"), convenience ("I/we *don't want* a baby right now"), or most insidiously, coercion.

This last reason is perhaps the most unacknowledged reason why many women undergo abortion. In a famous and well-regarded essay, Mary Meehan offers a number of reasons why "liberals" should stand against abortion.[5] Among her reasons is that contrary to pro-abortion feminist rhetoric, abortion is actually *exploitive* of women in many instances. "Many women are pressured by spouses, lovers, or parents into having abortions they do not want," she argues, "Sometimes the coercion is subtle, as when a husband complains of financial problems. Sometimes it is open and crude, as when a boyfriend threatens to end the affair unless the woman has an abortion, or when parents order a minor child to have an abortion."[6] Many of those who do so-called "sidewalk counseling," attempting to dissuade women on their way into abortion clinics from going through with the procedure, report that women who are accompanied to the abortion clinic by a husband or boyfriend often do not have the chance to stop and talk, because they are forced or hurried into the clinic

---

3. Alan Guttmacher Institute, *Induced Abortion, Facts in Brief,* 2002.

4. Ibid.

5. Meehan, "Left Has Betrayed the Sanctity of Life," 19–24.

6. Ibid., 23.

by their male partner. Women who come to the clinic by themselves are far more likely to talk and engage the counselors in conversation.

Another justification for abortion, this one usually employed under the guise of women's liberation and feminism, is that it is an issue of women's rights, autonomy, and self-determination. "My body, my choice!" the popular bumper sticker proclaims. This is at its core a classically liberal argument, appropriate in a country which is itself constitutionally founded on such classically liberal ideals as freedom, liberty, and independence. In order to contribute to feminism's stated goal of the full equality of women, it is argued that abortion on-demand is necessary for women to live as fully empowered and embodied selves, free from all responsibilities not freely chosen. But does a woman's seizing of exclusive authority over the fetus' life, as advocated by pro-abortion feminism, really contribute to feminists' stated goals of equality and autonomy? Sydney Callahan, a self-proclaimed "pro-life feminist," argues that on the contrary, permissive attitudes toward abortion actually *encourage* the continued victimization and exploitation of women by men:

> But if a woman claims the right to decide by herself whether the fetus becomes a child or not, what does this do to paternal and communal responsibility? Why should men share responsibility for child support or child rearing if they cannot share in what is asserted to be the woman's sole decision? Furthermore, if explicit intentions and consciously accepted contracts are necessary for moral obligations, why should men be held responsible for what *they* do not voluntarily choose to happen? By prochoice reasoning, a man who does not want to have a child, or whose contraceptive fails, can be exempted from the responsibility of fatherhood and child support. Traditionally, many men have been laggards in assuming parental responsibility and support for their children; ironically, ready abortion, often advocated as a response to male dereliction, legitimizes male irresponsibility and paves the way for even more male irresponsibility and lack of commitment.[7]

Callahan is one of a growing number of feminists who has begun to question the moral logic of connecting the liberation of women with the destruction of fetuses. "Women," she writes, "will never climb to equality and social empowerment over mounds of dead fetuses, numbering now

---

7. Sidney Callahan, "Abortion and the Sexual Agenda," 432–33.

in the millions."[8] The contemporary rights-oriented way of framing the abortion issue, employed by both sides of the debate is as morally repugnant as it is psychologically destructive, for it pits women in an adversarial relationship with their unborn children.

Additionally, feminist concern has traditionally been not only for women, but for *all* individuals and groups that have been subjugated and harmed by systemic oppression, violence, and exploitation. Should this not logically extend to the way in which feminists regard the growing child in the womb? "It is out of character for the Left to neglect the weak and helpless," Mary Meehan argues, because "the traditional mark of the Left has been its protection of the underdog, the weak, and the poor. The unborn child is the most helpless form of humanity, even more in need of protection than the poor tenant farmer or the mental patient or the boat people on the high seas."[9] Similarly, former Lutheran bishop Lowell Erdahl has argued that "True liberalism affirms the rights of the oppressed and stands for the protection of the weakest members of society, those who cannot defend themselves."[10] According to this line of criticism, by its direct attack on the most helpless and defenseless, abortion ironically undermines the very liberal and feminist values its advocates claim to be fighting for.

Ultimately justifications for abortion, as we will see with the other forms of justification of violence we will examine, involve the setting aside of the Christian presumption in favor of life in order that some lesser good might be pursued. Though as it has become clear, this lesser good is rarely, if ever, actually accomplished through the violence of abortion; as with all violence, it tends to only lead to more violence by those who have come to believe in the efficacy of killing as a means of social redress, as Dr. Tiller's murder and others like it have come to show.

---

8. Ibid., 432.

9. Meehan, "Left Has Betrayed the Sanctity of Life," 22.

10. Erdahl, *Pro-Life/Pro-Peace*, 36. Indeed, Erdahl sees "an inconsistency between being both a true feminist and an advocate of abortion rights. True feminism denies the right of any person to possess or control another" (35).

3

Justifications for Anti-Abortion Violence

THE NEXT STEP IN the cycle of violence we are exploring in the remainder of part 1, that of Dr. Tiller's murder and other violence against abortion providers, involves similar excuses and justifications for setting aside the human inclination not to take life. In this section, we will briefly explore the history of recent anti-abortion violence since the *Roe v. Wade* ruling, and then examine the stated rationale given by those who have killed abortionists and those who support those actions for why they believe deadly force is a legitimate means to combat the violence of abortion.

To be clear, the twisted logic of the murderous fringe of the anti-abortion movement is by no means representative of the movement as a whole. The major, mainstream voices of the antiabortion movement consistently and unequivocally denounce vigilante violence as an acceptable means of fighting abortion's violence. But just as every movement has its extremist fringe that potentially gives the movement's mainstream a bad reputation in the public conscience, antiabortion violence has been used continually by proponents of abortion rights to tarnish the image of the entire groundswell of abortion opposition in the public conscience. It is thus incumbent upon those who stand against the violence of abortion to understand the chilling ideology of those who would kill to "protect" life in this regard, in order to better confront and undermine the murderous ideology of violence in all its forms, as well as to make our own witness for life more effective, sound, and full of integrity.

The landmark 1973 *Roe v. Wade* ruling, striking down as unconstitutional all state laws banning abortions, sent a shockwave through American political and moral discourse. To some, the ruling was a vindication of feminist ideals and the dawn of a new era of "women's liberation." To others, the ruling was a grave assault on the "sanctity of life" by denying all value or moral legitimacy to the fetus independent of the whims of others. This latter group initially protested the wake of *Roe v. Wade* on secular grounds by appealing to the fetus' inherent "right to life," but as the 1980's began, such a rights defense had faded into the background as new, primarily religious voices came to the forefront in the battle against abortion.[1]

Coinciding with the overtly religious tone of the new face of the antiabortion movement, sporadic threats and actual occurrences of violence against abortion facilities began to occur, including death threats, bombings, fake anthrax letters, and butyric acid attacks, designed to frighten and intimidate abortion workers to leave their profession.[2] The extreme, shadowy fringes of the antiabortion movement showed that they were not against employing fear, destruction, and violence as "lesser evils," means toward the ultimate end of disrupting and reducing abortions.

Simultaneous with, but quite different in spirit from, this antiabortion terrorism and intimidation, Operation Rescue and similar mainstream groups staged massive blockades of abortion clinics, intended to disrupt the daily business of the abortionists through large-scale acts of nonviolent civil disobedience against what participants believed to be horribly unjust laws. These actions were distinct from, and opposed to using violence and fear as weapons in the struggle against abortion. Rather, Operation Rescue advocates saw themselves in the mold of nonviolent protests like André and Magda Trocmé's hiding of thousands of Jews from the Nazis in Le Chambon-sur-Lignon, France during World War II, or the bus boycotts, sit-ins, and other acts of nonviolent resistance by

1. Carol Mason's provocative book, *Killing For Life*, traces the rise of abortion violence directly to this religious discourse—calling abortion a "holocaust," "murder," an "abomination against God." She posits that what really drives the antiabortion violence of recent years is an apocalyptic rhetoric of millennialism, words which serve to radicalize otherwise moderate people with moral qualms against abortion. Mason's work is, not coincidentally, an excellent example of a pro-abortion medium which subtly attempts to paint the *entire* antiabortion movement with the same brush as the violent fringe. Through this "guilt by association" tactic, she ascribes the apocalyptic narrative she claims leads to violence to almost *all* abortion opponents, even those who condemn violence against abortion providers.

2. For a nuanced analysis of the history of antiabortion violence by the movement's extremist edge, see Fausset, "History of Violence on the Antiabortion Fringe." Fausset's article, unlike many less careful treatments of the subject, correctly points out that this violence is "carried out by a small minority of the much broader and generally peaceful movement that opposes abortion."

Martin Luther King, John Lewis, and others during the civil rights era. As a means of reinforcing this linkage, Operation Rescue organizers emphasized their commitment to nonviolence as a means of combating the violence of abortion. "Those participating in 'rescues' typically were required to sign a pledge card that, in the context of the overall purposes and goals of Operation Rescue, explicitly proscribes violence in any form."[3] One such pledge statement, from an Operation Rescue rally in Dayton, Ohio in 1997 reads in part:

> I understand the critical importance that this mission be unified, peaceful, and free of any actions or words that would appear violent or hateful to any witnesses of this event. I realize that some pro-abortion elements of the media may seek to discredit this event and focus on a side issue in order to avoid the central issues at hand: murdered children and exploited women. Hence, I understand that for the children's sake, this gathering must be orderly and above reproach. Therefore . . . I commit myself to be peaceful, prayerful, and nonviolent in both word and deed. Should I be arrested, I will not struggle with police in any way (whether in word or deed) but remain polite and not resist arrest, remembering that mercy triumph's [sic] over judgment.[4]

Deliberately attempting to distance themselves from those in the antiabortion movement who advocated violence, Operation Rescue at its height attracted tens of thousands of nonviolent protesters at rallies and clinic blockades, determined to fight against the evil of abortion's violence *without* using evil means.

However in 1992, Operation Rescue collapsed as an internally unified and cohesive organization, due to political struggles within the group's upper echelons, including Randall Terry's autocratic leadership style. The loss of a cohesive organizational structure led to anarchy within the movement with those advocating violence gaining more prominence in the media and therefore in the public eye. Further fueling radicalism, the Supreme Court upheld the essential findings of *Roe v. Wade* in *Planned Parenthood v. Casey*, only months after Operation Rescue's internal collapse.

Then, a new chapter began. On March 10, 1993, abortionist Dr. David Gunn was shot in the back and killed by Michael Griffin outside

3. Steiner, *Rhetoric of Operation Rescue*, 8.
4. Scanned image of Operation Rescue's "Return to Truth."

Gunn's Pensacola, Florida clinic. This was the first murder of an abortion provider by an abortion foe, and it enflamed the public debate like nothing before ever had. Popular sentiment turned rapidly against the antiabortion movement, and in the media and popular public discourse, there was no substantial difference between the nonviolent protests of Operation Rescue and Griffin's calculated murder. Quickly, a bill was introduced in the Senate called the Freedom of Access to Clinic Entrances (FACE) act, which when signed by President Bill Clinton in early 1994, made it a federal crime to block the entrance to abortion clinics or impede the daily business of any clinic worker or patient in any way, a backlash which denied the nonviolent Operation Rescue and like-minded groups their main channel of action and dissent. This backlash in turn may very well have contributed to the subsequent violence that quickly followed Dr. Gunn's assassination. According to a later editorial in the *Harvard Law Review* looking back on the antiabortion violence of the 1990's, in cracking down on the primary avenue of the antiabortion movement's nonviolent dissent, the FACE act had shut off one of the few remaining "safety valve[s]" for democratic dissent. Consequently, the editors wrote, as the government has "foreclosed nonviolent outlets of dissent, violence has increased."[5] The violent fringe of the antiabortion movement now felt even more compelled to act in ways the mainstream antiabortion groups had always condemned and which most contemporary antiabortion voices continue to do so.

On July 29, 1994, only months after the passage of the FACE act, a Presbyterian minister by the name of Paul Hill, fresh off media appearances in which he praised Griffin's murder of Dr. Gunn, shot and killed Dr. John Britton and his volunteer escort, James Barret with a shotgun outside the same Pensacola clinic at which Dr. Gunn had been murdered the previous year. Hill gave himself up to police immediately, and the following year was tried, convicted, and sentenced to death. We will return to Hill's story later in this section. Then in December of 1994, John Salvi opened fire in two Boston abortion clinics, killing two receptionists and wounding five other people. 1998 saw more fatalities committed by antiabortion extremists- including a clinic bombing by Eric Rudolph that killed a police officer and wounded several others, and the fatal shooting of Dr. Barnett Slepian in his home in a suburb of Buffalo, New York by

---

5. Cited in Shields, "A Time To Kill."

James Kopp. Though many analysts believed the wave of violence had crested, this is the trajectory into which Dr. Tiller's murder, which occurred over ten years after the last abortion-related murder, belongs.

The bombing of clinics and the killing of abortionists has in the past created backlash against the entire antiabortion movement and threatens to do so again in the aftermath of Tiller's murder. It has justifiably created a sense that those who claim to value life yet kill abortion doctors are unbelievably hypocritical. Counterdemonstrators opposed antiabortion advocates, chanting "Pro-life, you're name's a lie. You don't care if doctors die!" And in the eyes of many abortion advocates, the chronicle of abortion violence narrated above has "irrevocably connected the term pro-life with terrorism."[6] If we are to understand how to avoid this hypocrisy in our moral discourse, we must understand the distorted rationale of those who would hold this as an exception to the general presumption against killing. We turn now to briefly exploring *why* some people feel that killing those involved in abortion is justified.

Antiabortion violence is rooted first and foremost in the conviction that the fetus is a human life, the killing of which is morally equivalent to the killing of a born human being. This conviction is shared by many in the antiabortion movement, not only those who would resort to violence to oppose abortion. Yet it is only a small fraction of those who believe abortion to be an issue of violence who are themselves willing to kill in order to prevent it. Those who do find themselves willing to kill to stop abortion view abortion as among the worst abominations known to humanity, and as we saw with Randall Terry quoted above, frequently make comparisons between abortion and Nazi concentration camps or similar acts of mass murder. Therefore, they reason, if one would be willing to defend innocent human life using deadly force in other circumstances, how can the defense of innocent life *not* be justified in this instance? Killing an abortionist in order to stop him or her from killing innocent children is, to this line of reasoning, morally equivalent to killing a man threatening to blow up a school bus full of children.

In the wake of Michael Griffin's murder of Dr. David Gunn, a shadowy group known as the "Army of God"[7] released a "Defensive Action

6. Mason, *Killing For Life*, 2–3.

7. The Army of God is not so much an organization as it is a network of "leaderless resistance," or perhaps even a philosophy. Much like al Qaeda is today, it has no institutional leadership structure, but is instead a loosely-affiliated group of like-minded

Statement" in which the 29 signatories proclaimed their conviction that "all godly action necessary" to defend innocent life ought to be taken. Their conviction extended to the use of deadly force as well, for if there are ever circumstances in which it is justifiable to kill in defense of born human life, it is also justifiable to kill to prevent the destruction of unborn human life as well. "We proclaim that whatever force is legitimate to defend the life of a born child is legitimate to defend the life of an unborn child," the statement reads.[8] Following Paul Hill's murder of Dr. James Brittan and his escort James Barrett, the group issued a similar statement expressing support for these killings.[9] They condoned this violence by appealing to the principle of using violence to defend those who cannot defend themselves. One of Paul Hill's friends and supporters put it this way in a statement released after Hill's execution by the State of Florida in 2003:

> If we believe that an unborn child is just as much a "person" in God's sight as a born person is, then what Paul Hill did was DEFENSE, not "murder," not "retribution", not "taking the law into his own hands," not "vengeance." Simple defense. Loving your unborn neighbor as you love yourself. Being willing to lay down your life for an "innocent person in danger of loss of life or limb" as our common law describes "Defense of Another."[10]

This constant refrain of the theme of "defense" is deliberate- it suggests an appeal to the justifiable war trajectory of the Christian tradition that has been enshrined in international law and common social ethos.[11]

---

individuals, united in their fundamentalist Christianity as well as in their conviction that killing abortionists to prevent abortions is justified. Their website at http://www.armyof-god.com contains graphic pictures of aborted fetuses as well as numerous pages praising Paul Hill, Michael Griffin, James Kopp, and others who have killed abortion providers.

8. First "Defensive Action Statement," online at http://www.armyofgod.com/defense .html (accessed June 22, 2009). Tiller's alleged murderer, while not a signatory to the Defensive Action Statement, is reported to have been an admirer of the sentiments it expresses.

9. "Second Defensive Action Statement," online at http://www.armyofgod.com/defense2.html (accessed June 22, 2009).

10. Murch, "Eulogy for Paul Hill."

11. While this violence would fail the well-established just war criterion of "legitimate authority," since these individuals were not acting on behalf of a government or nation, the logic of the appeal is the same as that which legitimizes violence in a "just war," namely that it is legitimate to take up arms against an unjust aggressor or in order to defend innocent life which is being threatened.

Paul Hill, even before his own living out of this philosophy of "defensive action," was instrumental in formulating the theory behind the violent praxis. An original signatory to the first "Defensive Action Statement," Hill greatly elaborated on these convictions in a position paper called "Should We Defend Born and Unborn Children with Force?"[12] widely circulated among the radical fringe of the antiabortion movement. This paper is crucial for understanding the logic of those who would "kill for life," especially professing Christians, for Hill relies heavily on certain biblical paradigms in order to make his case. Hill's paper is composed of four main parts:

1. the biblical, ethical, and theological case for "defensive action,"

2. a section of "supporting authors" Hill cites as famous Christians who he believes would agree with him (including Thomas Aquinas, Martin Luther, John Calvin, Ulrich Zwingli, John Knox, George Buchanan, and Samuel Rutherford),

3. answers to ten objections that might be leveled against his case, and

4. a call to specific action for those who have been convinced by Hill's conclusions.

Through all this, Hill seeks to answer the guiding question "What responsibility does the individual have toward his neighbor if his neighbor's life is about to be taken by force?"

Hill's positive case begins with consideration of Scriptural paradigms which he believes enjoin Christians to kill to defend their own lives or the lives of the innocent. Citing Exodus 22:2, he concludes "the Bible clearly teaches that we may protect our own lives from unjust harm with deadly force if necessary." Thus, if we may (and perhaps, *should*) defend our lives with force, the second Great Commandment (Luke 10:27) necessitates that we love our neighbor as ourselves- including killing to defend our neighbor if necessary. Hill interprets Scriptural injunctions to protect innocent life as a license to do so violently if need be.

With this imperative as his driving principle, Hill next reckons with the reality that the government doesn't see it that way. By its failure to adhere to "God's law," requiring the defense of innocent life, by its tolerance

12. Currently available online at http://www.mttu.com/Articles/Should%20We%20 Defend%20Born%20And%20Unborn%20Children%20With%20Force.htm. Subsequent citations of this paper are from this source.

and protection of the practice of abortion, Hill claims that the United States government has abdicated its moral responsibility and therefore, its very legitimacy. In such circumstances when the authority of the government is no longer legitimate, the individual has an imperative to obey God's law and to oppose unjust human laws (Acts 5:29b). The divine imperative to protect innocent life trumps all human laws designed to prevent people from doing so, hence

> Individuals may, therefore, use force to deter a mass murderer who wantonly begins to kill innocent school children. Using the same logic, we may also use force against mass murderers who wantonly kill preschool and preborn children. We should do so even if some horribly unjust law presumes to declare it to be wrong to do so.

Fundamentally for Hill, the question comes down to the moral equivalency between the value of born and unborn human life. If one may kill to defend born human life, then one may also kill to defend human life that has not yet been born.

In his discussion of the "ethical basis for defensive action," Hill turns to the obscure and terrifying story of Phineas the priest in Numbers 25 for his paradigm. In the story, Israel is afflicted with plagues from the LORD because of the idolatry caused when some Israelite men were seduced by Moabite women into worshiping Moabite gods. God orders Israel to put to death any who had come to worship Baal through the Moabite influence. As Israel begins to weep at the idolatry and the realization of what they have been ordered to do, an Israelite man and his Midianite consort brazenly walk past the weeping assembly and into their tent. Phineas, son of Moses' brother Aaron, is said to be "zealous" for the honor of the LORD, and takes a spear and drives it through both the Israelite and the Midianite woman at once. Strikingly, the text has God commending Phineas for his zeal, and includes the promise of an eternal priesthood for Phineas' family (Numbers 25:10–13), and the plagues sent upon Israel cease.

In this strange story, Hill finds a hero worthy of emulation. He is struck by the way in which Phineas does not stop to ask Moses and the other leaders for permission, or the results of a due legal process, he simply takes the decree of God into his own hands. Citing John Calvin's commentary on this passage, Hill (an ordained Presbyterian minister) draws a number of principles in which he feels cases of lethal "defensive action" are warranted.

> Such an act must first arise from a pure motive. It must also be according to the legal standard found in the Bible and summarized in the Ten Commandments. Lastly, all such actions must ultimately seek the glory of God in order to be ethically justifiable. All true defensive action, therefore, must arise from the motive of love for God and our little neighbors. It must also be according to the objective law of God and seek the ultimate glory of God.

A justifiable "defensive action" must meet these criteria Hill maintains, whether it is done by agents of the government or by private individuals. Against the logic of the thinkers we will encounter in the next section who justify the violence of the state, but decry individuals carrying out such a sentence, Hill claims that "the responsibility to protect innocent life is not given directly to government leaders from God. This responsibility is first given to the people who delegate some of this responsibility to their appointed civil servants," a responsibility which becomes even more incumbent upon individuals when the government fails to protect innocent life.

In Hill's biblical interpretation, we can discern elements of the fundamentalist "flat book" approach to understanding the Bible. This is a simplistic way of reconciling the many contentious and even contradictory voices within the canon of Scripture. Rather than reading the Old Testament through the lens of the New, or through the person of Jesus Christ as the church has traditionally attempted to do, Hill's "flat book" methodology sidesteps all the thorny questions raised by the canon's inherent messiness and the relationship of the different parts of the canon to one another. Instead, it asserts them all as of equally normative value. Hence, the Phineas paradigm is asserted as normative alongside the "We must obey God rather than human beings!" paradigm of Acts 5:29 without regard for how the person and example of Jesus might alter the way we read and assign varying degrees of authority to the differing voices within the scriptural witness.

One of Hill's responses to objections raised against "defensive action" is worth exploring, because it further shows Hill's lack of a developed interpretive strategy for reading the Bible. In responding to the objection that the example of Jesus' nonresistance in the face of the government that put him to death should preclude violent resistance, Hill interprets the example of Jesus very narrowly: "Christ had a direct command from God that he should offer His life as an atoning sacrifice. His case was unique. We have no such command. We have the God-given responsibility to take defensive action to protect life." By asserting Jesus' nonviolent suffering servanthood as a non-normative "unique" case, Hill has conveniently avoided the single biggest impediment to Christian participation in violence. Jesus' teaching and life are thus marginalized in Hill's interpretive framework as special.[13] Christians must instead look elsewhere for our moral guidance. By contrast, in part 2 we will see that for the early Christian church, conformity to the example of the incarnate Jesus is a vital part of Christian discipleship and was the fundamental reason they rejected human bloodshed.

Hill's thinking on this matter has a chilling consistency about it. We may summarize his argument briefly in the following propositions:

1. If the killing of unborn children through abortion is morally equivalent to the murder of children who have been born,

2. If it is one of the highest human moral imperatives to defend innocent children from a killer by killing the killer if necessary,

3. And if the government is failing in its responsibility to protect innocent lives through its sanctioning of legalized abortion,

4. Then killing an abortionist to defend his unborn victims is a righteous action.

Hill himself challenged his readers to act consistently—asserting that more Christians who call themselves "pro-life" ought to be willing to kill as he was in order to defend innocent human life. "The reason abortion began and has not ended yet," Hill explained, "is due to our inconsistent

---

13. The early Christian church certainly didn't see things Hill's way. 1 Peter cites the nonretaliatory suffering of Jesus as an example to be emulated: "To this you were called, because Christ suffered for you, leaving you an example, that you should follow in his steps" (1 Peter 2:21, TNIV). Where Hill sees Christ's death as a unique, non-repeatable commission to Jesus and Jesus only, Scripture and the early church see in the cross a moral paradigm to be emulated by all those who would take up their cross to follow as Jesus' disciples. This is an essential point which cuts directly to the heart of what it means to be Christian, calling the standard Christological definitions asserted by the ecumenical councils into question if they are not tied into an ethic of obedience to and imitation of Jesus as the normative human being. As John Howard Yoder provocatively asked in *Politics of Jesus*, "What becomes of the meaning of the incarnation if Jesus is not normatively human? If he is human but not normative, is this not the ancient ebionitic heresy? If he be somehow authoritative but not in his humanness, is this not a new gnosticism?" (10).

thinking and action." If abortion is murder, and we would normally be willing to kill an unjust aggressor to stop murder from occurring, then why are we not willing to kill to stop abortion from killing the innocent children? In the main body of this book, we will hear the voices of some Christians who would take up such a call for moral consistency in the ancient Christian church, but in a radically different way than Paul Hill would have envisioned. Now, we turn to understand the voices of those who would justify killing by the state as a response to murder, and the exceptions against the rule proscribing the taking of human life which these voices postulate.

4

Justifications for State-Sanctioned Violence

JUST AS THE VIOLENCE of abortion and the "defensive action" violence against abortion providers have their proponents, the third "moment" in this cycle of violence also has its advocates, many of whom condemn the violence of the first two moments. As in the first two moments, this final moment involves making exceptions against the general rule against taking human lives which its advocates feel are justified. Because, as of this writing, the case against Dr. Tiller's alleged murderer is still in its early phases, it is unclear whether Scott Roeder will actually face the death penalty in the state of Kansas, and no one is as of yet vocally calling for his execution, although as with Paul Hill, it remains a distinct possibility. So, rather than focusing on the many sophisticated arguments by supporters of the narrow issue of the death penalty, as we did with abortion supporters and "defensive action" proponents, here we will seek a broader understanding of the viewpoints of those who would reject both the first two moments in our cycle of violence, and yet embrace and even laud the violence of the state as the third moment when violence is given its most "legitimate" expression.

In the wake of George Tiller's slaying, the Internet was abuzz with antiabortion activists attempting to distance themselves from the rationale and tactics behind Tiller's killing, some of which we have already seen. What was it about Tiller's slaying that caused so many of Tiller's opponents to denounce it? Was it a tactical decision based in shrewd political calculations about the backlash that would occur against the antiabortion movement? For some it clearly was. Even Paul Hill had acknowledged in his essay cited in the previous chapter that there should be a distinction made between the "wisdom" of killing an abortionist and the "justice" of doing it; the latter he staunchly defended, the former he acknowledged was open to interpretation and debate given the circumstances.

Was it an opposition to violence in principle? Again, this is certainly the case for some abortion opponents. For example, Elizabeth Scalia, writing in the blog of the religion, culture, and politics journal *First Things*, decried Tiller's murder because "Tiller, despite his choices, was still a created creature of God, and his life was God's to take, not man's," and in cutting off Tiller's soul before it had its chance at repentance in Christ's good time and mercy, the killer may have imperiled his own soul. Further, "When we start thinking that we know the heart and mind of God so well that we may decide who lives and who dies, we slip into a mode of Antichrist."[1] This conviction that human life is God's and not ours to take will show up again soon as we dive into the words and witness of the ancient Christian church.

Rather, the reason most abortion opponents condemn Tiller's murder is neither a consequentialist political calculation, nor an opposition to violence in principle, but a sincere conviction that Tiller's murder was an instance of inappropriate violence because it was carried out by the *wrong agent* in the *wrong circumstances*. Drawing upon the just war criteria of "legitimate authority," which generally forbids those who are not exercising properly held authority from engaging in violence, this point of view essentially rules out all vigilantism. The only right use of force is by such a duly constituted authority, whether that authority be a police officer or soldier or other agent of the government. It rules out retribution by "private" individuals or groups not acting in an official capacity from the government. In this view, the state essentially has a monopoly on the use of force.

In a textbook example of this essentially politically conservative philosophy, Creighton University theology professor R. R. Reno, also writing on the *First Things* blog,[2] explains why in his view the actions of Tiller's murderer were morally unjustifiable. Citing Cardinal Joseph Rigali of Philadelphia's statement that the United States Catholic Bishops' Conference denounces "all forms of violence in our society," Reno calls the cardinal's general condemnation of violence "a bit overboard" and "unhelpfully expansive." Why? Because not all killing is wrong. There are a number of restrictions the conventionally accepted wisdom of the Christian tradition has imposed on just who may be killed by whom,

1. Scalia, "Tiller, Long, Bonhoeffer, and Assassination."
2. Reno, "Defending Life Requires Law."

including an absolute prohibition on the "intrinsic evil" of intentionally killing innocent people, and proportionality restrictions on the use of force teach us that "Killing of any sort is wrong if it is not necessary for the protection of life." But the chief criterion Reno is concerned with in this instance is that of "legitimate authority." He asserts that though we have a right to self-defense, and a duty to protect others, yet somewhat paradoxically, when it comes to a calculated, premeditated use of force, "no individual can take justice into his or her own hands."

Thus, according to Reno, the reason Tiller's killing as it occurred was morally wrong was not because Tiller was innocent (he was not), not because the use of force was disproportionate, but because "his killer was acting as the law unto himself. He arrogated to himself the roles of jury, judge, and executioner. He violated the principle of legitimate authority." Where does this legitimate authority come from? In the Christian tradition, Reno argues, the Bible stresses the legitimate authority principle a great deal. St. Paul is "especially emphatic" on this point in Romans 13. Here is Romans 13:1 as Reno cites it:

> "Let every person be subject to governing authorities," *and not just now and then, but in every respect,*[3] "for there is no authority except from God, and those authorities that exist have been instituted by God."

Note here Reno's editorial comment on Paul—that this injunction is not just a conditional, time-bound mandate to be subject to the governing authorities, but is instead an absolute, universal command permitting no exceptions—"and not just now and then, but in *every* respect." By his reading of Paul, the governing authorities have been established by God for the good order of society, that evil might be restrained through the use of force. This emphasis on God's providential establishment of governments to do us good is also the basis of the medieval notion of the divine right of kings, in which obedience to specific rulers is enjoined because God has chosen that specific ruler to serve in that capacity.

Reno's analysis of the situation surrounding Tiller's murder, and his articulation of the importance of the "legitimate authority" principle leaves one very large question unaddressed however. What about the "We must obey God rather than human beings!" paradigm of Acts 5:29? Paul Hill and those few who urge violence against abortion providers take this

---

3. My emphasis added.

principle to heart, for implicit in it is a conviction that there is a moral law higher than the law of the land. This was the conviction that drove Hill and Tiller's killer, that obedience to God always trumps obedience to human authorities when the two are in conflict. This conviction drove not only the violent fringe of the antiabortion movement, but also the nonviolent civil rights movement of the 1950's and 60's in their struggle against the racist Jim Crow laws and institutionalized segregation imposed by these same "legitimate authorities." What does one do if the "legitimate authorities" are fundamentally corrupt? Reno does not address this question. Without some very important qualifications which he neglects to provide in this piece, Reno's argument would legitimate *all* governments.

According to Reno's view, in which the legitimate authorities alone are invested with the right and duty to use force to combat evil, the violence of the state is properly construed as retribution rather than vengeance. The difference between the two in this mindset is subtle but important. As Carol Mason explains, "Vengeance is akin to revenge and counterattack. Retribution, in contrast, seeks to restore social order based on particular principles."[4] That is, motivation is the key distinction. Vengeance is seeking to address a wrong—a personal grievance, a settling of a score, a sense of revenge or payback. Retribution, by contrast, is based in the desire to restore social order in the face of a perceived wrong; by this thinking, retribution serves to seek the greatest good for the social order. A just war or capital punishment meet these requirements as the only legitimate use of force—retribution for the good of the social order. As Notre Dame law professor Charles E. Rice put it in an essay written in the wake of the first killings of abortionists in the 1990's, "Apart from the just war, capital punishment, or the justified rebellion, which derive from the authority of God, no one may ever intentionally kill anyone."[5]

DECONSTRUCTING A BAD READING OF ROMANS 13

This standard, popular view, which has been developed since the time of Augustine in the fourth century, is in Christian discourse premised on a certain reading of Rom 13:1–7, which as we have seen, Reno leans on quite heavily in making his case. This crucial biblical passage has been called upon time and time again to support an essentially conservative

4. Mason, *Killing For Life*, 72.

5. Rice, "Can the Killing of Abortionists Be Justified?"

political worldview. The astute observer will recognize four broad characteristics of this reading of Romans 13:1–7 and subsequent political philosophies and theologies that ground themselves upon it, all four of which are implicitly present in Reno's argument:

1. There is a generally positive view of the "governing authorities." This includes positive affirmations of the vocation and calling of the governing authorities, and appreciation for their role in maintaining order through the violence of the sword.

2. The belief that the powers that be are "established," "ordained," "instituted," or otherwise "set up," by God.

3. Resisting the authorities via insurrection, civil disobedience, or noncompliance is sinning against what God has established.

4. The major interpretive trend is to remove 13:1–7 from its context, isolating it from the crucial material in chapter 12, and essentially making this pericope into a stand-alone short treatise on the authority of the state.

In what follows I will proceed exegetically through the crucial portions of 13:1–7, delving into the text to bring to light some of the grammatical nuances missed by the vast majority of our contemporary English translations that have perpetuated the unfortunate conservative misreading of this contentious pericope. We will find that not only can the four characteristics noted above *not* be legitimately derived from the biblical text, but also that Paul's message to the Romans is fundamentally grounded in a subversive trust in the God who has *triumphed* over the very powers to which the Christians are to be subordinated.[6] I must begin this exegesis however, by challenging one of the dominant interpretive trends that keeps Christians in bondage to this stagnant, conservative reading.

The most significant interpretive trend we must challenge is that of decontextualizing Romans 13:1–7 and reading it as if it were a complete

---

6. The message is essentially the same as that of the old spiritual, "He's Got the Whole World in His Hands": Christ, the world's *true* "authority," has defeated the powers of darkness (including the governments) which hold the world in bondage. Those who belong to him therefore need not stoop to their level and rebel against the authorities' evil and violence using evil or violent means, but as 12:21 exhorts right before 13:1–7, they should seek to "overcome evil with good," just as Christ has.

literary unit. Romans 13:1–7 cannot function as a stand-alone theology of the state because, quite frankly, it does not stand alone. It is intricately tied in with what precedes it and what follows. This passage comes in the middle of the ethical exhortation section of Paul's letter—in light of the theological claims he has laid out in chapters 1–11, chapters 12 and 13 provide Paul's answer to the question of how to live. Further supporting this contextual reading is the fact that Romans 13:1–7 is bookended by discussions about suffering love (12:9ff., and 13:8–10). Thus, any discussion of 13:1–7 which is not also read in light of its surrounding context of Christlike suffering love must be rejected as a misinterpretation. We will maintain this awareness of the context of 13:1–7, as well as its place within the larger Pauline corpus as we proceed in our commentary. Readers who wish to follow this exegesis closely are advised to have their favorite English translation of the Bible opened to Romans 13:1–7 in order to compare notes.

13:1a: *Pasa psychē exousiais hyperechousais hypotassesthō*

Literally: *(Let) every soul (be) under-ordered to the over-having authorities . . .*

Paul begins with an exhortation that every *psychē* or "soul"[7] must be "subordinated" to those authorities. Two key points on Paul's choice of vocabulary must be borne in mind as we proceed. First, the verb in this clause is an imperative-a command—in the passive voice. *Hypotassō* is a prefix-augmented variant of the verb *tassō*. *Tassō* is crucial for 13:1–7, because it occurs repeatedly in several forms throughout this passage. It means "order," as in straightening up, controlling the chaos, arranging, maintaining the proper state of things. Combined with the prefix *hypo* (meaning "under"), it means in 13:1 "be ordered under," or *voluntarily* permit your order to be sublimated to that of the authorities. This is no passive submission to the authorities. It means allowing the authorities' "order" to exist on top of one's own "order."[8] Concretely, this would mean for the Roman church to which Paul is writing that they must either obey the commands of the authorities *where Christian conscience permits*, or they must disobey the authorities where obeying would be a violation of

7. This word carries the Hebraic sense of personhood, not the Platonic sense of the disembodied soul.

8. N. T. Wright puts it this way: "The word has echoes of military formation: one must take one's place in the appropriate rank." "Romans," 720.

Christian conscience—but then they must be *willing to accept the consequences* of that disobedience. To be "ordered under" does not imply obedience in all circumstances; rather it means *not rebelling* against the order which is over top of you. Verse two will make this point more explicitly.

The other point from this first clause that must be remembered is that the *exousiai* ("authorities") did not merely connote human authorities for Paul and his audience as we often assume today in our rush to identify these idealized "authorities" with our own political masters. The discussion of the authorities needs to be situated into the much larger discussion of what has come to be known in theological shorthand as the "powers and principalities."[9] In the Greco Roman milieu, "the boundaries between the spirit world and the world of humanity and nature were fluid and often imperceptible."[10] In the worldview into which both Paul and his Roman audience (not to mention everyone else in Rome) were socialized, spirits infused everything and had untold influence on events of the physical, material realm. Understanding of, and even *sympathy to* this point is utterly crucial for a proper comprehension of to whom or what Paul enjoins subordination. Clinton Morrison puts it forcefully:

> If we are to be a party to Paul's communication with the Roman church in Rome we must enter into a world in which we cannot make radical distinctions between myth and history, material and spiritual, as we do today. It was a well known fact in antiquity that the same word was used, not only to indicate 'both' spiritual and material elements, but to symbolize the inseparable relationship between the spiritual and material worlds.[11]

The point is that in addition to the human *exousiai* we moderns so quickly read into the text, Paul also has in mind the underlying spiritual reality and the forces *behind* the earthly powers and principalities, rulers and authorities. As N. T. Wright comments, it is unlikely that Paul

9. For more on the "powers and principalities" language in the Bible and its theological ramifications for contemporary discourses of resistance, see Walter Wink's excellent *Powers* trilogy: *Naming the Powers: The Language of Power in the New Testament*, *Unmasking the Powers*, and *Engaging the Powers: Discernment and Resistance in a World of Domination* (Fortress, 1984, 1986, and 1992 respectively). The theologian who is widely credited with bringing the "powers and principalities" language back into vogue is William Stringfellow in his *An Ethic for Christians and Other Aliens in a Strange Land* (Waco, TX: Word, 1973).

10. Morrison, *Powers That Be*, 99.

11. Ibid., 98.

ever made a clean distinction between the earthly and heavenly dimensions of civic authority, even if here the human elements are emphasized predominantly.[12]

What does Paul have to say elsewhere regarding the powers and principalities that stand behind the *exousiai*? Elsewhere in Romans (8:38–39), Paul displays his contempt for the *archai* and *dynameis* ("rulers"[13] and "powers") which he says are utterly impotent in the face of the love of God in Christ Jesus. Likewise, and even more forcefully, in Col 2:15, Paul[14] declares that Christ has "disarmed[15] the rulers and authorities (*archas* and *exousiai*) and made a public spectacle of them, triumphing over them in it."[16] Again and again, Paul tells us that the powers have been rendered impotent and defeated by Christ, and that they, in their service of darkness and death, no longer have the last word. *These* are the implications the word *exousiai* would have carried for Paul and his Roman readers. Thus, even though the powers and authorities have been disarmed and robbed of their sting, Christians are still to be "subordinated" to them. To find out why, we must read on in Romans 13.

> Romans 13:1b: *Ou gar estin exousia ei mē hypo theou, hai de ousai hypo theou tetagmenai eisin.*
>
> Literally: *for there is no authority except* under *God, and those that are (or, exist) are ordered* under *God.*

The prepositions are crucial in this clause. The twin use of *hypo* here hearkens back to the connotation of "order" we observed above. It is not the agential use, in which case we would translate it "by," as in most modern English translations. Paul declares that no authority presently existing has *not* been "ordered" *under* God. The participle *tetagmenai* is another form of *tassō*, which we noted above means "order," or "set into place." Countless generations of English translations have lost this sense,

---

12. Wright, "Romans," 720.

13. Compare with Romans 13:3, which also speaks of the "rulers."

14. Either Paul, or the person writing in Paul's name and authority. From a canonical point of view, it makes no difference.

15. The Greek word here connotes essentially rendering them absolutely impotent, despoiling them.

16. The "it" here refers back to the cross in Colossians 2:14. The implement of torture, humiliation, and shame has thus become the means of conquering evil and disarming the insidious powers that killed Jesus and continue to kill him today.

instead translating the participle as "ordained" (KJV), "established" (NIV), or "instituted" (NRSV). The difference is crucial. John Howard Yoder puts it this way:

> God is not said to *create* or *institute* or *ordain* the powers that be, but only to *order* them, to put them in order, sovereignly to tell them where they belong, what is their place. It is not as if there was a time when there was no government and then God made government through a new creative intervention; there has been hierarchy and authority and power since human society existed. Its exercise has involved domination, disrespect for human dignity, and real or potential violence ever since sin has existed. Nor is it that by ordering this realm God specifically, morally approves of what a government does. The sergeant does not produce the soldiers he drills; the librarian does not create nor approve of the book she or he catalogs and shelves. Likewise God does not take responsibility for the existence of the rebellious "powers that be" or for their shape or identity; they already are. What the text says is that God orders them, brings them into line, providentially and permissively lines them up with divine purposes.[17]

Here is the key point at which the conservative reading of Romans 13 misses the mark. This observation puts the lie to all claims that the civil authorities are a providential creation of God. Thus, what Paul is saying here is not that we must subordinate ourselves to the governing authorities because God set them up to rule over us—rather, we are to be subordinated to them because they themselves have been brought under God's control. They are, in effect, "ordered under" God because of what Christ has done in disarming the powers. Unbeknownst to the powers, God uses them unwittingly, unjust and perverted as they may be, to powerfully bring about the fulfillment of his divine plans.[18] In the same way he used the brutality of the armies of Israel and those of Israel's enemies for his redemptive purposes throughout the Old Testament, so too even the idolatrous might of the Roman Empire could be held in its proper place by God.

---

17. Yoder, *Politics of Jesus*, 201–2.

18. The story of Joseph in Genesis beautifully encapsulates this principle. God worked through the evil done to Joseph by his brothers in order to bring about a great deliverance. As Joseph says, "You intended to harm me, but God intended it for good to accomplish what is now being done, the saving of many lives" (Gen 50:20).

Romans 13:2a: *Hōste ho antitassomenos tēi exousiai tēi tou theou diatagēi anthestēken*

Literally: *So then the one who is ordered-against the authority stands against the order of God . . .*

In verse two, the emphasis on order continues unabated. *Antitassomenos* is a participle combining "anti" with *tassō* for a combined word literally meaning "order against." The person who allows him or herself to be "ordered against" the authority (instead of "ordered under," as in verse 1) is consequently standing against the "order" of God. *diatagēi* is simply a noun form of *tassō*. It is God's *order* which is being resisted by the one who orders herself or himself against the authorities, since they themselves have been ordered under God because of God's saving actions in the Christ event. Setting one's own order in opposition to the order God has brought about is idolatrous, and as the second half of the verse goes on to say, will incur judgment.

Reading further into the passage, and here we must recall that the context of Rom 13:1–7 explicitly includes Rom 12:9–21 and 13:8–10 as well, another textual observation enables us to further clarify the role of human government in God's plans. The government is used providentially by God to restrict evil so that his people can live faithfully with at least a modicum of safety. 13:4b reads "He is God's servant, an avenger (*ekdikos*) of wrath (*orgēn*) to bring punishment on the wrongdoer." These words are important, because looking back in the passage, 12:19 explicitly denies the prerogative of vengeance and violence to God's people using the same words: "Do not take revenge (*ekdikountes*), my friends, but leave room for God's wrath (*orgēi*), for it is written: 'It is mine to avenge (*ekdikēsis*); I will repay,' says the Lord." Several observations follow from the identical vocabulary usage in these two verses, so close to one another in the passage. (1) The Christian is denied the prerogative of revenge. This is because, as the quote from Deut 32:35 in Rom 12:19 makes clear, vengeance belongs to the Lord alone, and to take vengeance and violence into our own hands without explicit sanction from God is to transgress the boundaries God has imposed on human morality. (2) 12:19 says to "leave room for God's wrath (*orgēi*), and 13:4b relates that the governmental exercise of coercion is one of the modes through which God exercises his wrath (*orgēn*). (3) The unnamed ruler in this passage is God's "servant," and designated "avenger" (*ekdikos*). Thus, the function that is forbidden for Christians is said to be exercised by the rulers.

It will not do, as the tradition since Augustine has suggested, to posit the denial of revenge to be binding on Christians in the sphere of "private morality" while claiming that Christians acting as governmental agents are *required* to carry out God's vengeance in the sphere of "public morality." This is because such dualistic designations are the product of philosophical innovations attempting to confine religion's applicability only to one's "private" life. Similarly, Martin Luther's "two kingdom" theology had the unfortunate effect of planting the unbiblical notion that Christians can serve two masters simultaneously[19] at the very heart of Reformation theology. These thought patterns are entirely foreign to the world of the biblical writers. Rather, the message Paul is sending here is clear—Christians are to have nothing to do with the coercive violence of the state. State violence is in God's providential hands, "ordering" and controlling the violence of human beings, but it is not a function to be engaged in by Christians. Yoder, comparing the two verses we have just examined, puts it this way,

> It is inconceivable that these two verses, using such similar language, should be meant to be read independently of one another. This makes it clear that the function exercised by government is not the function to be exercised by Christians.[20]

That God can take the evil of human beings and turn it around for his own glory and the outworking of his providential purposes is not in dispute; indeed, we see it at work as far back as Joseph's recognition of this fact in Gen 45:5–9 and 50:20. What we must come to realize is that Romans 13 was written *with this idea explicitly in mind*. While God uses the evil of state violence to *restrict* the domain of human evil in the world, the vocation of the Christian church is not to fight evil through these evil means; rather we are called to *transform* evil into good with the prophetic voice of the Word of God and the suffering love which he modeled for us.

---

19. Matt 6:24. While Luther claimed that both spheres of morality, both "kingdoms" as it were, are ultimately in the service of God, if this is the case, how can it be that the same Master would demand such diametrically opposed courses of action based on whether one is wearing his or her "Christian hat" or "official government hat," so to speak?

20. Yoder, *Politics of Jesus*, 198.

Or, as Paul puts it, "Do not be overcome by evil, but overcome evil with good" (Rom 12:21).

Further discrediting the nationalistic reading of Rom 13:1–7 is a simple historical observation. This passage has often been invoked by both skeptics and naïve Christians alike as justification for a simplistic view of blind obedience to the state, but it is hard to imagine a more flagrantly decontextualized reading of this passage. The nameless "authority" Paul speaks of in Romans 13 is not some idealized ruler, setting forth the vision of what government ought to be like in a perfect world. The "authority" is, concretely, the despotic pagan emperor Nero, with whom the Christians of Rome would have been intimately familiar. The fact that Paul calls Nero God's "servant" is especially significant. For Paul, it puts him firmly within an established Jewish tradition that recognized God's use of his "instrument" Assyria in Isaiah 8, or his use of his "servant" Nebuchadnezzar (Jer 27:6), or his "anointed" (i.e., literally, "messiah"—Isa 45:1), Cyrus. In the Hebrew Scriptures, God frequently uses pagan kings and armies to accomplish his wrathful purposes, and this is precisely the function Paul is alluding to by calling the despotic emperor Nero God's "servant" in Rom 13:1. That very same "servant" would later put Paul to death during the terrible persecution in Rome in the mid to late AD 60's.[21]

21. The Roman historian Tacitus gives us an account of what went on in Rome in the mid 60's under Nero. The great fire of AD 64 had devastated the large portion of Rome, and popular sentiment, not without justification, pointed the finger of blame at Nero himself for starting the fire. "Consequently," Tacitus reports, "to get rid of the report, Nero fastened the guilt and inflicted the most exquisite tortures on a class hated for their abominations, called Christians by the populace. Christus, from whom the name had its origin, suffered the extreme penalty during the reign of Tiberius at the hands of one of our procurators, Pontius Pilatus, and a most mischievous superstition, thus checked for the moment, again broke out not only in Judaea, the first source of the evil, but even in Rome, where all things hideous and shameful from every part of the world find their centre and become popular. Accordingly, an arrest was first made of all who pleaded guilty; then, upon their information, an immense multitude was convicted, not so much of the crime of firing the city, as of hatred against mankind. Mockery of every sort was added to their deaths. Covered with the skins of beasts, they were torn by dogs and perished, or were nailed to crosses, or were doomed to the flames and burnt, to serve as a nightly illumination, when daylight had expired Nero offered his gardens for the spectacle, and was exhibiting a show in the circus, while he mingled with the people in the dress of a charioteer or stood aloft on a car. Hence, even for criminals who deserved extreme and exemplary punishment, there arose a feeling of compassion; for it was not, as it seemed, for the public good, but to glut one man's cruelty, that they were being destroyed" (Tacitus, *Annals*, 15.44, online: http://old.perseus.tufts.edu/cgi-bin/ptext?lookup=Tac.+Ann.+15.44).

While Nero may or may not have yet reached the heights of his psychosis by the time Paul wrote his letter to the Romans, recent memory would have reminded the Romans of the madness of Caligula and the despotism of Nero's other predecessors. They too, are affirmed as God's unwitting "servants." In this context, Rom 12 and 13 function as "a call to a nonresistant attitude toward a tyrannical government. This is the immediate and concrete meaning of the text; how strange then to make it the classic proof for the duty of Christians to kill."[22]

The conservative reading of Romans 13:1–7 has resulted in, on one hand, the legitimization of totalitarian regimes by imperial apologists of all stripes, and on the other hand, the dismissal of Pauline thought as hopelessly outmoded and naïve by liberal interpreters. It has been the goal of this section to demonstrate that it is not Romans 13 itself which is to blame, but the unfortunate misreading of Romans 13 which has occurred on all sides of the ideological spectrum. Some of this is due to the accidents of history, others to malicious exploitation of the biblical text and those who value it. Christians can no more cut Romans 13 out of the canon than we can rid ourselves of our annoying "in-laws": both are part of our family and our heritage. As Wright puts it in his discussion of this pericope, "Exegesis, and the determination to live at least with its results, and perhaps even by them, is always a risk, part of the risk of an incarnational religion or faith."[23] We must reclaim Romans 13 from both the tyrants and the cultured despisers, and read it with fresh eyes as it truly is, not through the mistaken interpretive lenses bequeathed to us by the centuries. Doing so may well help us discover a *new* "two kingdoms" theology, one which recognizes the fallen nature of the kingdom of the "powers that be," and seeks to overwhelm them with the light of the inbreaking kingdom of God.

22. Yoder, *Politics of Jesus*, 202–3.
23. Wright, "Romans," 716.

5

The Need for Consistency

IN OUR EXPLORATION OF the aftermath of George Tiller's murder and the cycle of violence of which it is a part, we have observed that in each of the three moments we have looked at, there are those who believe that killing in one of the instances is justified, while in the other two, it is not. For advocates of abortion, killing the child in the womb is justifiable provided that it is done for the betterment of the life of the mother. For proponents of "defensive action" killing an abortion doctor is permissible as long as the goal is to defend the innocent life in the womb. And for those who stress the violence of the state, killing is permissible provided it is done by one endowed with "legitimate authority" for the purpose of defending life.

Members of each of these three groups would all say that they oppose killing in most circumstances, and in a way, would say that they are "pro-life."[1] Yet each group also clearly condones killing in certain instances. What then, does the label "pro-life" mean, if each group finds itself willing to kill mutually exclusive groups of people under contradictory circumstances? Each group is pro-life, but only if human life is defined conditionally and contingently. The major societal debate is thus not whether killing human beings is right or wrong, but under which conditions it is morally permissible to kill. Each group accuses the others of hypocrisy and inconsistency while warding off similar charges by the others. What would it take to achieve some moral consistency?

1. Even many of those who advocate "abortion rights," call themselves "pro-life." Witness the work of Dr. Leonard Peikoff, president of the Ayn Rand Institute and legal heir to the philosopher's estate, who in an essay entitled "Abortion Rights are Pro-Life" unabashedly asserts that "Abortion-rights advocates should not cede the terms 'pro-life' and 'right to life' to the anti-abortionists. It is a woman's right to her life that gives her the right to terminate her pregnancy." Online: http://www.abortionisprolife.com/abortion-rights-are-pro-life.htm.

Many voices cry out for this consistency. Some of these voices come from the most unlikely of people- the moral claims of whom few are likely to be interested in listening to. Take an Islamic terrorist for example- Ramzi Ahmed Yousef, the mastermind of the 1993 World Trade Center bombing that killed six people and injured more than 1,000. What could he possibly have to say regarding the moral life which he so clearly disregarded with his murderous act? Yet for all his moral failings, Yousef himself showed a surprising amount of integrity as he owned up to the label of "terrorist." "I am a terrorist," he told the judge during his trial, "and I am proud of it as long as it is against the U.S. government and Israel."[2] But Yousef also claimed that he was not alone in his terrorism. Turning the accusation on its head, Yousef leveled the charge at his American captors:

> Well, you were the first ones who invented this terrorism . . . when you dropped an atomic bomb which killed tens of thousands of women and children in Japan . . . You killed them by burning them to death. You killed civilians in Vietnam with chemicals . . . You went to wars more than any other country in this century, and then you have the nerve to talk about killing innocent people. . . . You keep talking about solving problems by peaceful means and peaceful ways. You are the people who stand in the way of peaceful means and peaceful ways.[3]

"You are butchers and terrorists yourself," he told the riveted courtroom. Yousef assailed the hypocrisy of those who denounced the killing of innocent people with truck bombs, and yet killed innocent people themselves by dropping bombs out of airplanes. To those on the receiving end, is it any more wrong when a "terrorist" does it than when a "legitimate authority" does it?

Another surprising voice making a similar charge comes from Timothy McVeigh, the man primarily behind the 1995 bombing of the Alfred P. Murrah Federal Building in Oklahoma City that killed 168 people, including 19 children and infants in the building's daycare center. In June 1998, while McVeigh was in prison awaiting his execution, a short essay appeared in *Media Bypass* magazine bearing McVeigh's name.[4] Written at a time of heightened tension between the United States and

2. Goldman, "Bomb Plot Architect Gets Life Term."

3. Cited in Kavanaugh, *Who Counts as Persons?*, 115.

4. McVeigh, "An Essay on Hypocrisy." The essay was later proven to be genuine.

Iraq that ultimately led to a period of American air strikes and cruise missile bombardments of Iraq, McVeigh derides as "hypocrisy" the American public's condemnation of his bombing of the federal building while offering moral approval for the bombardment of government facilities in Baghdad and throughout Iraq. "What motivates these seemingly contradictory positions?" he asks. "Do people think that government workers in Iraq are any less human than those in Oklahoma City? Do they think that Iraqis don't have families who will grieve and mourn the loss of their loved ones? In this context, do people come to believe that the killing of foreigners is somehow different than the killing of Americans?" The mode of the bombing, McVeigh argues, whether by truck or suicide belt, missile or airplane makes no difference to those on the receiving end. To McVeigh, the morality of the two actions is comparable: "Whether you wish to admit it or not, when you approve, morally, of the bombing of foreign targets by the U.S. military, you are approving of acts morally equivalent to the bombing in Oklahoma City." Then referring to the famous photograph in the aftermath of the Murrah building bombing of the fireman holding the dying child, he adds, "The only difference is that this nation is not going to see any foreign casualties appear on the cover of *Newsweek* magazine."

All this is obviously not to suggest that Ramzi Yousef and Tim McVeigh are paragons of wisdom and virtue, for they are cold-blooded killers. However, what they do possess is a kind of refreshing candor and integrity, in that they do not dodge or hide the fact that they are killers and terrorists. And like the rest of those who justify killing in the name of some greater or lesser cause, they've proven by their actions that they believe there are exceptions to the rules against killing human life. Where their voices are most pointed however is in their confrontation of killing by the "legitimate authorities." Yousef and McVeigh challenge us to step back from behind the euphemisms ("collateral damage," "termination of pregnancy," etc.), the depersonalization of the victims, and the illusion of moral high ground, and to come face-to-face with the reality of our actions, with the human face of those we have killed in the name of national security, social stability, retribution, or "choice."

In order to show that this line of criticism is no mere whim of madmen, I turn to the voice of one of America's contemporary saints whose life reflects an authenticity and integrity to the moral principles he taught to the public. On the 4th of April, 1967, exactly a year to the day before he was assassinated, Dr. Martin Luther King Jr. addressed a gathered meeting of Clergy and Laity Concerned, a religious coalition assembled to oppose the policies of the Johnson administration in Vietnam. This particular evening, King was not speaking on equal civil rights or race relations, as had been his wont for over a decade; he had come at last to break his silence on the American war in Vietnam. Relating his decision to finally "come out" publicly against the war, King explained that it was intimately tied up with his work on behalf of civil rights and racial justice. While counseling those who wanted to use violence to advance the cause of equal rights against their actions, King was asked why *they* shouldn't when the United States government was using massive violence to advance its own interests in Vietnam. In effect, why can the empire do it with all its massive military might, while we who are powerless and voiceless can not?

"Their questions hit home," King admitted, "and I knew that I could never again raise my voice against the violence of the oppressed in the ghettoes without having first spoken clearly to the greatest purveyor of violence in the world today—*my own government*."[5] Consistency demanded that as a Christian leader, King could no longer preach nonviolence in the struggle for racial justice while remaining silent in the face of the violence perpetrated by those whose employment of destructive force and killing power was exponentially greater than that of those who had been trampled underfoot. Being consistent means being just as honest about your *own* failings and the evils of your allies, nation, friends, etc. as you are about the evils of those you oppose.

PREPARING TO KILL

We have already seen how advocates of the three moments in the cycle of violence, of which George Tiller's murder is a part, specifically justify their positions and the rationale for when human life becomes expendable or forfeitable. Now, we need to take a step back and look at one of the most important metajustifications that serves as a prerequisite for nearly all forms of violence—depersonalization of the proposed victim. It is my contention that dehumanizing someone, robbing them of their human dignity and worth in our thoughts and in our actions, is the first

---

5. King, "Time to Break Silence," 233 (emphasis mine).

necessary step along the demonic path that may ultimately lead us to the killing that person.

We as human beings are naturally endowed with an instinct against killing those of our own kind. This instinct may be suppressed, denied, or conditioned out of us, but it seems to be hard-wired into our individual moral compasses. For example, an official Army historian and widely-respected military analyst, S. L. A. Marshall conducted a study of the fire rates of combat soldiers during World War II. His results challenge the popular conception of soldiers as dispassionately doing their duty when they kill an enemy. Marshall found that of all the soldiers in combat zones who had opportunity to fire their weapons at the enemy, "on an average, not more than 15 per cent of the men had actually fired at the enemy . . . The best showing that could be made by the most spirited and aggressive companies was that one man in four had made at least some use of his fire power."[6] The sheer fact that three fourths of U.S. Army World War II soldiers would not fire their weapon at the enemy given the opportunity to do so, even though their own lives were in danger in the combat zone, suggests an innate hesitancy toward killing deeply imbued in human nature.[7]

The Army was of course quite unnerved by this study, and took great pains to rectify the situation in future wars through vigorous training and conditioning of combat soldiers.[8] One technique, called "reflexive fire training" teaches soldiers to fire quickly, as bypassing the normal process of moral reasoning through intense behavioral conditioning. The World War II-era round bull's-eye shaped targets were replaced with human-shaped targets, and soldiers were taught to fire on sight so that firing

6. Marshall, *Men Against Fire*, 54. Marshall's work, originally published in 1947, has been challenged on methodological grounds, but his results have largely been accepted by the U.S. military and serve as a baseline for their efforts to increase fire rates in subsequent wars.

7. For more on this point, see Lt. Colonel Dave Grossman's *On Killing*. Grossman explores Marshall's results and finds them to be fundamentally sound, concluding that the extraordinarily low firing rates during World War II were due primarily to "the simple and demonstrable fact that there is within most men an intense resistance to killing their fellow men. A resistance so strong that, in many circumstances, soldiers will die before they can overcome it" (4).

8. For this discussion, I am indebted to the information in the 2008 documentary "Soldiers of Conscience," released by Luna Productions, about conscientious objectors within the military ranks during the present Iraq war. Information on the film can be found at http://www.socfilm.com.

their weapon became second-nature, or reflexive. In this way, the Army gradually increased the fire rates in the following wars, so that it grew from World War II's 25 percent, to 55 percent in the Korean conflict, to upwards of 80 percent in Vietnam. In modern conflicts, such as in Iraq, the fire rate is well over 90 percent as the training soldiers receive works hard to condition the suppression of the innate instinct against killing.

This program of reflexive fire training serves to enshrine in practice what is necessary in thought to prepare a person to kill another human being—the depersonalization of the victim. "Today, any human being is a candidate for elimination, from someone's perspective," writes moral theologian John Kavanaugh, "The tactic takes one of two forms: Either exclude such humans from our definition of meaningful or 'full' person-hood or, if forced to accept them as persons, justify the killing of them in the name of a greater good or more pressing value."[9] Kavanaugh's observation underscores what we have seen to this point, and pushes it out even further: Under the multiplicity of theories and ideas that exist in the world about what killing is legitimate and morally permissible, *no one* is completely free from consideration as a target in this nefarious calculus.

Because of this deeply ingrained presumption against killing, on the rational level, decisions to kill have come to be understood as exceptions. "We should never kill another human being," we tell ourselves, "*unless* . . . he is a murderer . . . her life is not worth living . . . the baby will have Down's Syndrome . . . the civilians just lived too close to that enemy bomb factory . . ." None of us embrace *all* of these exceptions, but most people embrace at least some of them. As Kavanaugh comments,

> Every perpetrator of every outrage has had good reasons and im-
> portant causes for every death: to defend my life, my name, my
> property, my family, my heritage, my race, my nation, my religion.
> In each case, some moral "absolute" often is invoked—but never
> the absolute value of human life. Instead . . . the absolute claim of
> some *other* interest that allows the killer an *exceptionalism* unites
> the logic of the terrorist with the logic of the respectable nation.[10]

When we decide that some lesser good, be it security, convenience, retribution, or good old-fashioned selfishness, overrides the prime value of the unique human life we propose to extinguish, we find ourselves

9. Kavanaugh, *Who Counts as Persons?* 3.

10. Ibid., 114 (emphasis original).

at the cusp of the infamous slippery slope—once we begin the journey downward, it is very difficult to arrest ourselves from free-fall. If we use the millions of abortions as justification for a murder this time, then the next time an unpleasant situation comes up, it will be all the easier for us to find rationale for other murders. If we use the horrific worst-case scenarios to justify abortions, we risk sliding too easily into a culture that doesn't bat an eyelash at over a million abortions annually, most of which occur for far less reason than the worst-case scenario we had legislated for in the first place. If we embrace a preemptive war doctrine against Iraq out of fear of immanent attack by weapons of mass destruction, we will be far more likely to fall in behind the next time a President urges us to war at the next "national emergency" that is given to us via slick sales pitch. Once one exception for "justifiable homicide" is permitted, where is the line drawn? Who arbitrates what is acceptable, even laudable killing, and what is morally reprehensible?

The most efficient way to overcome our human inclinations against killing another human being is to redefine the personhood out of them— to reduce the target of our violence into a thing rather than a person, a "what" rather than a "who." In an illuminating book on the word play necessary to accomplish this insidious end, William Brennan identifies eight categories of dehumanizing designations those proposing to kill apply, consciously or unconsciously, to their intended victims:

1. *deficient human* (stupid, defective, inferior, potential life, lives not worth living)

2. *less than human* (subhuman, nonhuman)

3. *animal* (beast, lower animal)

4. *parasitic creature* (parasite, vermin, lice)

5. *infectious disease* (pestilence, plague, epidemic, infection, contagion)

6. *inanimate object* (thing, property, material, merchandise)

7. *waste product* (trash, rubbish, debris, garbage, refuse)

8. *non-person* (social, psychological, or legal nonexistence)[11]

11. Brennan, *Dehumanizing the Vulnerable*. Brennan's chart, "The Semantics of Oppression," appears in the back of this book as Appendix C, 128–29. Brennan's work documents the insidious parallelism in the dehumanizing rhetoric of those who justify the oppression and killing of groups of vulnerable victims, including Native Americans, African Americans, enemies of the former Soviet Union, European Jews, women, unwanted unborn human life, and the disabled.

Each of these categories can be detected in the rhetoric of the approval of killing or other kinds of violence. The Nazi regime, for example, routinely employed categories five and seven (among others) in the run-up to the mass murders of the Holocaust. For many years in the American experience, black slaves were counted and valued as three-fifths of a person, a clear employment of category two. Soldiers in Vietnam routinely dehumanized their Vietnamese enemies with the racial slur "gooks." Category eight, among others, is even now frequently utilized to deny the humanity of human persons prior to their births in order to make the taking of their lives more palatable and socially acceptable. The examples could be multiplied, but experience has shown that routine depersonalization of an individual or group leads to a devaluation of their personal existence, making it increasingly likely that they may be the target of violence.

Killing is only the final stop, frequently the logical conclusion on this demonic road of depersonalization. When we kill, we rob the victim of her personhood—the animus, personality, experiences, mind—in short the very *life* that defines who she is. Kavanaugh reminds us that "the most definitive and irreversible way to turn a person into a thing, to reduce a person to an object, to negate existing personal reality, is to kill a person."[12] Quite literally, killing ontologically turns a person into an inanimate object, a corpse.

Given violence's dependence on dehumanizing thoughts and rhetoric then, it seems that the most effective way to combat violence is not by fighting the "bad violence" of the world's evildoers with the righteous violence of the "good guys," but rather to go straight to the root of the matter by standing up against all forms of depersonalization. In doing so, we may cut off the seeds of violence before they are allowed to germinate into full-blown killing. The courage of those who stand up against dehumanization, both of themselves and of others, even in the face of intense public and social pressures to conform to the dominant depersonalizing social narratives, is the single greatest way to fight violence and to begin to create the kind of world in which all may have the chance to flourish. Brennan notes that

> historically, one of the main reasons for the decline in or termination of oppression against various peoples and groups has been the presence of individuals who, even during periods when the

12. Kavanaugh, *Who Counts as Persons?* 119.

discrediting semantics predominated, refused to accept the prevailing norms of name-calling. The success of any genuine human rights campaign rests in large part on the capacity of its proponents to forge positive, personalized, and exalted images of the victims as worthwhile human beings whose oppression can no longer be tolerated.[13]

The duty of those of us who would call ourselves "pro-life" then is clear- we must stand up for justice and for the humanity of those whom society deems expendable. We must stand in solidarity with the human casualties of our government's decisions to rain death down from the sky. We must confront those who would justify the destruction of a human fetus with the truly human face of the victim of abortion's carnage, asserting that we have an obligation to ensure that she too has a full human career as an embodied person. Equally, it is also our responsibility to stand against all prejudices, attitudes and social structures that devalue people based on any characteristic, real or imagined, including age, sex, race, (dis)ability, physical attributes, ideology, political alignment, guilt or innocence, sexual orientation, wealth or poverty, social status, religion, nationality, or any other qualification that has been employed in the past to construe an individual or group a lesser human being (or less fully human) than ourselves. This is the way in which we can begin to recover *our own* humanity as we stand up to defend the humanity of our neighbor from all delegitimizing and dehumanizing rhetoric and actions.

CONSISTENTLY PRO-LIFE

Given that, as we have seen, many different groups and people claim for themselves the label of "pro-life," yet justify killing in different, mutually exclusive circumstances, what would it take to develop an ethic that is consistently pro-life across the board? On what basis might it be grounded? Historically, there have been two main ways in which advocates of consistency in ethics have attempted to unite such seemingly disparate moral issues as abortion, war, capital punishment, poverty, and racism under a banner of the protection and flourishing of human life: secular natural law tradition and, what we may call a Christian "divine law" tradi-

13. Brennan, *Dehumanizing the Vulnerable*, 18–19. Brennan documents examples of such refusals to accept the prevailing dehumanizing narratives by portraying groups of vulnerable victims as fully human, as well as spiritual persons created in God's image. See his "Lexicon of Esteem," Appendix B (125 in this book).

tion. Both of these traditions have value, and despite their quite different ways of getting there, both arrive at the same conclusion that intentionally killing a human person is morally indefensible.

In the natural law tradition, represented most clearly in our contemporary world in Roman Catholicism, the innate human instinct against killing is taken as a general moral imperative. While many natural law theorists would claim that some exceptions to this imperative are regrettable, yet morally defensible, others would not. Jesuit John Kavanaugh, whose work we have already encountered above, is an excellent example of the latter. Grounding his ethic in the inherent value of human persons, who possess genetic individuality and unique gifting and endowments (whether or not these endowments are fully actualized), Kavanaugh maintains that the fact that each person (even identical twins) is a unique and irreplaceable individual renders the human person inviolable, never to be killed intentionally. Leaning heavily on Thomas Aquinas, Kavanaugh argues that "the moral universe is grounded in the intrinsic constitution of human persons," and "humans, by the very fact of being human, are endowed with the intrinsic value of personhood" (p. 93, 103). Human beings and our endowed freedom of conscience and choice, are the reason moral value, good and evil, right and wrong, truth and beauty, exist- because we alone among all the earth's creatures possess the ability to ascribe value or lack of value to the things of our world. Our value is intrinsically in who we *are*, and not what we *do*. Kavanaugh thus emphatically rejects "performance-based" theories of personhood based on what a person does or cannot do. As a result, Kavanaugh's work is ultimately aimed at defending "the extremely controversial position that intentionally killing a human person is never ethically permissible" (p. 4).

What I will call the Christian "divine law" tradition agrees with the outcome of this line of natural law reasoning, but heartily differs in how that conclusion is reached. For a Christian reader, notably absent from Kavanaugh's formulation is any reference to God. What is God's relationship to this system? Did God create humans persons to be "intrinsically inviolable?" Rather, this tradition begins its moral discernment theologically rather than anthropologically. If human life is, as the natural law tradition posits, intrinsically valuable, why has the Christian tradition valued martyrdom as a faithful expression of Christian discipleship? Stanley Hauerwas has argued this point forcefully in a passage worth citing at length:

Well, I want to know where Christians get the notion that life is sacred. That notion seems to have no reference at all to God. Any good secularist can think that life is sacred. Of course what the secularist means by the word *sacred* is interesting, but the idea that Christians are about the maintenance of some principle separate from our understanding of God is just crazy. As a matter of fact, Christians do not believe that life is sacred. I often remind my right-to-life friends that Christians took their children with them to martyrdom rather than have them raised pagan. Christians believe there is much worth dying for. We do not believe that human life is an absolute good in and of itself. Of course our desire to protect human life is part of our seeing each person as God's creature. But that does not mean that we believe that life is an overriding good.

To say that life is an overriding good is to underwrite the modern sentimentality that there is absolutely nothing in this world for which it is worth dying. Christians know that Christianity is simply extended training in dying early.[14]

If not for the notion of intrinsic value, or the sacredness of human life, one may ask, why should Christians not kill another human being? What is the rationale? For the divine law tradition, the prohibition rests in the fundamental conviction that human life is simply not ours to take. Theologically speaking, we are radically dependent on God for everything, and continue to exist moment-to-moment not out of any inherent goodness or merit of our own, but on the sheer unmerited grace of God, a free gift from One who has and is everything to those of us who have and are nothing. God alone is the author of life, and only God may withdraw that gift. Killing a human person then, is to usurp into our misguided hands the right and prerogative that belongs *only* to God.

As a Christian theologian and ethicist, I am more persuaded by and attracted to the divine law tradition as represented by Hauerwas than the natural law tradition as represented by Kavanaugh. To complete Hauerwas's thoughts, I believe that there are many things worth dying for in the suffering love of Jesus, but nothing worth killing for. To me, nothing is worth the idolatry and presumption of taking into my hands that which only God may give. Remember the words of St. Paul, urging the Roman Christians to never take violent revenge on their enemies or persecutors—"Do not take revenge, my dear friends, but leave room for

14. Hauerwas, "Abortion, Theologically Considered," 231.

God's wrath, for it is written: 'It is mine to avenge; I will repay,' says the Lord." (Rom 12:19, TNIV). Paul draws upon the Hebrew Scriptures in Deut 32:35 to underscore the reason followers of Jesus should not avenge themselves violently, and the church rests on this principle.

I am not alone in these convictions. Instead, I position myself within the moral trajectory of the Christian tradition that rejects all forms of violence against human beings. This trajectory has been a vocal, yet distinctly minority position since the Christianization of the Roman Empire under the watchful eye of the emperor Constantine and his successors in the fourth century. But before this massive compromise between church and state, the effects of which we are still suffering in the twenty-first century, it was decidedly the majority position, enjoying widespread support in all geographical corners of the church as the "unofficially official" moral stance of the body of Christ. In fact, as I will attempt to show in part 2, *no surviving orthodox Christian writing dating from before Constantine* ever *approves of Christian participation in human bloodshed.*

In the rest of this work, I will *not* be attempting a systematic and airtight formulation of the theological and philosophical underpinnings for such an ethic—that is the province of saints and specialists with far more training and expertise than I yet possess. Instead what I offer you, the reader, in part 2, the main body of this work, is the fruits of my historical research into the ethical and moral formation of the early Christian church. Specifically—what did ancient Christians, those closest in time and cultural context to the apostles, think about killing?

PART TWO

The Ethics of Bloodshed
in Ancient Christianity

6

Recovering an Ancient Church Teaching

CHRISTIANITY IS NOT MERELY a worldview, or a belief system; it is also fundamentally a way of life that demands obedience to the teaching and moral example of Jesus Christ. As Christians, we worship a God who emptied himself of heavenly glory for a time, in order to walk among us, talk with us, teach us, and show us how to live. His life culminated in an ugly, painful, and shameful death on the cross at Golgotha, a death which was simultaneously the means for the salvation of the world, and the culmination of a life of suffering love of neighbor and obedience to God. As such, the cross stands as our moral paradigm—the ultimate example of laying down one's life for one's friends (John 15:13). Reflecting on the significance of the cross, 1 Peter 2:21 tells us that we were called to a life of redemptive suffering, "because Christ suffered for you, leaving you an example, that you should follow in his steps."

But how is a Christian, whose life is manifestly dedicated to suffering love for the sake of others, to respond to the evil and violence of the world? Since the fourth century, when Constantine, Ambrose, Augustine, and others cemented the ethos of the imperial church into the mindset of global Christianity, it has been readily assumed that killing another human being in certain circumstances is *not* inconsistent with the way of the cross. The justification of violence has been shoehorned into the gospel ethic through all manner of elaborate contrivances and prooftexts.

Yet it has not always been thus. Prior to the seismic shift in social status that occurred when the emperor Constantine put an end to the persecution of Christians in the fourth century, and the subsequent actions of his successors in turning the faith into the official religion of the Roman Empire, the church's attitude toward bloodshed was markedly different, as was its relationship to imperial power. In this study, I shall explore the social ethic of the pre-Constantinian Christian church with respect to the question of the permissibility or impermissibility of taking human life in various circumstances.

This project had its genesis in the research for my master's thesis, *Proclaiming the Gospel of Peace: Living Faithfully According to the Original Vision*, completed in 2007 for Eastern Mennonite Seminary in Harrisonburg, Virginia. In that work, I researched the attitudes of the early church toward peace and justice, presenting overall trends and lifting up specific representative documents which demonstrated the countercultural and overall nonviolent nature of the early Christian moral outlook. A theory began to suggest itself to me—it seemed that no matter which century, or which part of the empire, every author that I encountered from before Constantine seemed to denounce human bloodshed in a variety of contexts, from abortion, to killing in war, and everything in between, espousing and living what may be termed a *consistently pro-life* ethic. This project is my attempt to comprehensively flesh out this thesis.

The conclusions of the scholarly literature surrounding the subject of the early church's attitude toward military service are as multifarious as the scholars conducting this research. Attempts to describe an overall pattern have come to *pacifist* conclusions,[1] decidedly *anti-pacifist* conclusions,[2] and conclusions that fall somewhere in between.[3] Indeed, so much research has been done into the question of the early church's attitude toward military service over the past 120 years, that Peter Brock of the University of Toronto was able to compile a nearly 20-page bibliography detailing all the books, journal articles, and other studies that had been conducted into the question until 1987,[4] with the pile of literature on the question growing still larger ever since. Generally, these studies have focused on the narrow questions of the church's blessing or condemnation of military service, and the number of Christians serving in the Roman legions during the era in question. As a result, the issue has usually been isolated from the early Christians' general ethical framework, much to the detriment of our common knowledge of that period.

In this study, I seek to broaden the issue and to explore the possibility of an overall moral stance against the shedding of human blood

1. E.g., Cadoux, *Early Christian Attitude to War*; Bainton, *Christian Attitudes toward War and Peace*; and Hornus, *It Is Not Lawful for Me to Fight*.

2. Most notably in the works of John Helgeland, e.g., "Early Church and War," 34–47.

3. E.g., Swift, *Early Fathers on War and Military Service*.

4. Brock, *Military Question in the Early Church*.

by Christians. The early church fathers and mothers left us no scarcity of literature to explore, and much of it pertains directly to the moral life envisioned by the gospel of Jesus Christ. Over the course of my research, I have been reading nearly every extant orthodox Christian letter, apology, and treatise dating from before Constantine's Edict of Milan in 311, in order to draw some definitive conclusions. Because the amount of literature is vast, I had to set some limits to my quest.[5] First, I limited my reading mainly to those writers whose teachings church tradition has held to be mostly orthodox, thus excluding Gnostic writings, for example. Second, I needed to eliminate apocryphal gospels and the numerous pseudonymous apocalypses, except where directed to them by primary or secondary literature. Finally for the sake of brevity and to keep the task before me manageable, I was forced to skip the many volumes of straight biblical commentary by writers such as Origen. Beyond those limitations, I believe I accomplished my goal of reading every primary source document dating from before 311. The works were all read in translation, however I made sure to seek out the newest and best translations of each document, as the classic Roberts-Donaldson *Ante-Nicene Fathers* collection is nearly 150 years old and is now archaic and inadequate at many points. Most came from the *Ancient Christian Writers* series, published by Newman Press, and the *Fathers of the Church* series, published by Catholic University of America Press. I cite them as they appear in these scholarly translations; though most of them were done before the use of gender-inclusive language for humanity became widespread, so I beg the reader's pardon at this point.

In presenting my findings here, I will organize them topically, categorized by subject. For each topic discussed here, I present some representative samples of comments made by the bishops, theologians, apologists, and martyrs that help demonstrate the attitude of the church at large. Where there appears to be disagreement or nuances between the thinking of particular writers or schools within the church, I note and analyze these. The first topic to look at is abortion and infanticide. I group these two together because, as will become clear, in the thought of the early church, there was no difference between killing a baby before it was born or after it had been born. Secondly, I explore the church's extant remarks on the bloodsport of the spectacles of the Roman arena, including gladi-

---

5. My complete reading list can be found at the end of this book as Appendix A.

atorial matches, chariot races, and public executions. Third, I offer a few brief remarks made by the fathers of the church concerning suicide, the taking of one's own life. Fourth, I turn my attention to the contentious issue of military service and killing in war, the subject of so many studies over the past century. I seek to connect this issue with the church's larger moral framework by relating it to these other issues, so that it does not remain an isolated and decontextualized historical inquiry. Fifth, by way of synthesis, I analyze a series of unambiguous, categorical statements by the early church which declare in no uncertain terms the immorality of killing human beings in any shape whatsoever and the incompatibility of violence with the gospel of life. This section serves to draw together the various threads we will have observed to that point into a cohesive whole. Sixth, after examining how the early church would *not* respond to evil (i.e., through violence), I turn my focus to the church's positive, constructive response to evil—through the virtue of *hypomonē* (Greek) or *patientia* (Latin). These two words convey similar, if not identical concepts in their respective languages—longsuffering, patient endurance, and waiting on God for his promised vindication rather than asserting that vindication yourself. This virtue finds itself enshrined most clearly in the Sermon on the Mount and in the Pauline injunction to abstain from revenge, the prerogative of which belongs to God alone (Rom 12:19). Seventh, I bring forward up a number of passages which demonstrate that the early church believed itself to be living the partial fulfillment of the eschatological promises of peace and nonviolence foretold by the prophets, especially Isa 2:1–5. Eighth and finally, I close with the early church's attitude toward martyrdom, indicating that while they were profoundly unwilling to *kill*, they were more than willing to *be killed* bearing witness to their faith in and loyalty to Jesus Christ. These eight considerations demonstrate a consistent pattern of renunciation of violence and the shedding of human blood (except of course, for their own) in the teaching and lived praxis of the early church.

Overall, we will see an emerging pattern of profound reverence for human life as the invaluable creation of a loving God. Athenagoras, writing in the second century about how the inestimable worth of the human life demands that God fulfill his promise of incorruptibility and bodily resurrection, declares that God "created man for the sake of the life of man the creature, a life not to be kindled for a brief space and then snuffed out" (*The Resurrection of the Dead* 12). As a result of this inestimable worth, in the words of one early fourth century writer, "in this command of God, no exception whatsoever must be made. It is always wrong to kill a man whom God has intended to be a sacrosanct creature" (Lactantius *Divine Institutes* 6.20). These startling sentiments, so far removed from our contemporary Constantinized Christian social ethic that permits the slaying of "sacrosanct creatures" if done in the name of "justice," "national security," or "choice," we will find are the norm, rather than the exception in the ethos of primitive, preimperial Christianity. The message of the early church is for Christian disciples today is one which calls us back to the *consistently* pro-life way of the cross.

7

Killing Our Children: Abortion and Infanticide

T HE FIRST TOPIC AT hand is the practice of killing unwanted children. Michael Gorman's excellent survey on the topic of abortion in
antiquity[1] catalogues the frequency and high degree of legitimacy and
cultural sanction given to it by the Greco-Roman world in the first several
centuries CE. As it had been for the Greeks, the killing of unwanted or
deformed infants (whether in the womb or after birth) was commonplace
in Roman society. Abortion was practiced for both reasons of popula-
tion control (primarily among the poor), but also for cosmetic reasons
among the rich who often wanted to preserve their "sex appeal."[2] Infants
were commonly subject to the practice of exposure, in which they were
simply abandoned on a rural mountainside to die.[3] Abortions of unborn
infants were carried out almost as frequently, using a number of mechani-
cal or chemical[4] means. In Greek and Roman law, all rights, including the
right to life, "were subservient to the welfare of the state (or the family,
the religion, or the race) and had to be sacrificed if the best interests of
the state demanded it."[5] Roman law, especially as codified in the Twelve
Tables, recognized the father of the family, the *paterfamilias*, as head of
household. For the *paterfamilias*, "his slaves, wife, and children were all

1. Gorman, *Abortion & the Early Church*.

2. Ibid., 15.

3. Greek dramatist Sophocles' play *Oedipus Rex* relates the story of a tragic hero who
had been left to die of exposure as an infant. Few in Sophocles' audience would have
batted an eyelash at the morality of this common cultural practice.

4. The various herbal compounds and recipes which had been discovered to be abor-
tifacient by Greco-Roman physicians were generally called "poisons" throughout the
ancient literature (see ibid., 15). It seems quite plain that they realized they were killing a
human being, they just didn't care.

5. Ibid., 23.

'taken in hand,' *mancipia*, to him, and he had the power of life and death, *jus vitae necisque*, over them all. The *paterfamilias* could kill, mutilate and sell people like posessions."[6] Against such a backdrop, the slaughter of Bethlehem's boys as ordered by Rome's puppet king Herod (Matthew 2:16) is not such an inscrutably large leap. Gorman's comments aptly sum up the moral situation throughout the empire at the time of Jesus:

> When Octavian (later called Caesar Augustus) appeared on the political scene, the Roman Republic was in disastrous moral and economic straits. The practice of abortion, which had reached an unprecedented height in the first century BC, remained at a high rate throughout that century and the next.[7]

In stark contrast to this culture of disposability, the early Christians asserted that the God-given inviolability of human life forbid them from taking the life of a child, either while still in the womb, or after birth. This prohibition is present from the very earliest strata of postcanonical Christian tradition to well beyond the "church peace" of Constantine. First, from the late first-century discipleship manual known as the *Didache*, or "The Teaching of the Twelve Apostles to the Nations," we find a categorical prohibition of abortion and infanticide included as part of the "way of life" section: "A further commandment of the Teaching: Do not murder; do not commit adultery; do not practice pederasty; do not fornicate; do not steal; do not deal in magic; do not practice sorcery; do not kill a fetus by abortion, or commit infanticide" (*Didache* 2.1–2).[8] Similarly, the *Didache* includes among those who follow the "way of death" "murderers of children, destroyers of God's image" (5.2) which must, by the document's chiastic structure, be understood as the antithesis of the command in chapter 2.

Such an explicit command was necessary because of the prevalence and acceptability of abortions and infant exposures in that era. The Christian character Octavian, in Minicius Felix's early third-century dialogue of the same name, was one of many apologists who responded to the common charge leveled against Christians by their pagan critics that Christians kill and eat their offspring in their secretive worship services.

---

6. Ibid.

7. Ibid., 26.

8. The "Two Ways" section of the Didache is closely mirrored in the *Epistle of Barnabas*, where a nearly identical prohibition of abortion and infanticide is present in chapter 19.

"And in fact," he retorts, "it is a practice of *yours*, I observe, to expose your very own children to birds and wild beasts, or at times to smother and strangle them—a pitiful way to die; and there are women who swallow drugs to stifle in their own womb the beginnings of a man to be—committing infanticide before they give birth to their infant" (*Octavius* 30). In another apologetic passage addressed to the emperor Marcus Aurelius refuting the pagan charge that Christians kill children, Athenagoras replies with a blistering demonstration of the consistency of the Christian pro-life ethic:

> Again, we call it murder and say it will be accountable to God if women use instruments to procure abortion: how shall we be called murderers ourselves? The same man cannot regard that which a woman carries in her womb as a living creature, and therefore as an object of value to God, and then go about to slay the creature that has come forth to the light of day. The same man cannot forbid the exposure of children, equating such exposure with child murder, and then slay a child that has found one to bring it up. No, we are always consistent, everywhere the same, obedient to our rule and not masters of it. (*Embassy for Christians* 35)

The great second century apologist Justin Martyr likewise reflects the Christian condemnation of this practice, saying that "we have been taught that to expose newly born infants is the work of wicked people" (*First Apology*, 27) while Clement of Alexandria laments that "women who resort to some sort of deadly abortion drug kill not only the embryo but, along with it, human kindness" (*Christ the Educator* 2.10).

Some of the arguments church leaders advanced against the practice of abortion in those early years sound remarkably similar to arguments used by abortion foes in modern America. For example, Tertullian's treatise on the soul contains a striking assertion, which, although it was one of his last works, written during his Montanist phase, nonetheless exhibits the early church orthodoxy which can be observed in other writers of his day as well. "Now we believe," he writes, "that life begins at conception, since we hold that the soul begins to exist at that time; for where life is, there must be a soul" (*On the Soul* 27.3). How frequently do we hear the phrase "life begins at conception" bandied about in contemporary debates about abortion? Far from being a recent innovation in the culture wars, this claim is nearly as ancient as the church itself. Building off this assumption of ensoulment at conception, Lactantius, too, protests vigorously against abortion: "Let no one, then, think that it is to be conceded even, that newly born children may be done away with, an especially great impiety! God breathes souls into them for life, not for death. Yet men, lest they stain their hands with that which is a crime, deny light not given by them to souls still fresh and simple . . . These are without any question criminal and unjust" (*Divine Institutes* 6:20). And Origen, in his eighth book responding to the pagan critic Celsus, insists that when Christians marry, God "certainly requires us to bring up the offspring and not to destroy the children given by providence" (*Against Celsus* 8.55). Finally, Tertullian's brilliant *Apology*, among his earlier works, contains a powerful indictment of another argument employed by abortion proponents—both today and in Tertullian's day—that the aborted fetus is only a "potential human."

> But with us, murder is forbidden once for all. We are not permitted to destroy even the fetus in the womb, as long as blood is still being drawn to form a human being. To prevent the birth of a child is a quicker way to murder. It makes no difference whether one destroys a soul already born or interferes with its coming to birth. It is a human being and one who is to be a man, for the whole fruit is already present in the seed. (*Apology* 9)[9]

Indeed, from the evidence we have observed here, the early church spoke with univocal passion and conviction that the abortion of a baby in the womb or the killing of one who had already been born were nothing short of murder. The two practices we now tend to separate based

9. We should not let the fact that the ancients (Christians included) were unaware of the woman's contribution of genetic material to the developing baby distract us from their rationale for opposing abortions. In the ancient world, it was believed by many that the male seed contained the entirety of the genetic material necessary for the development of the human fetus, and the woman was usually conceived of as a passive incubator for the growing child. Now we know that the woman herself contributes 50 percent of the child's DNA. This advancement in medical knowledge however cannot legitimately be construed as an excuse for setting aside the ancient Christian opposition to abortion as "backward" or "ignorant"—the origin of the child's DNA is irrelevant to the issue, because it is the existence of the child's life that the ancient Christians recognized (but some today do not) that is the crucial matter under consideration in these passages.

To ask the question "Is the fetus a person?" is equivalent to the Pharisee's self-justifying question "Who is my neighbor?" (Luke 10:29). For just as the Pharisee wanted to know whether he was exempt from his responsibility as a Jew to care for his neighbor by defining "neighbor" in a narrow, exclusionary way, the one asking the question of the fetus' humanity or "personhood" seeks to justify him- or herself by avoiding the responsibility as a human being to care for a fellow human being by defining personhood in an equally exclusionary way.

on our sensitivity to our brothers and sisters with "pro-choice" leanings, were indistinguishable to our Christian forbearers who resoundingly rejected child-killing, either in its prenatal or postnatal forms. Indeed as Richard Hays has remarked, "the recent shift in some branches of liberal Protestantism to advocacy for abortion rights is a major departure from the church's historic teaching."[10] The voices of the early saints convict us in our moral laxity and unfaithfulness to Christ.

10. Hays, *Moral Vision of the New Testament*, 453.

8

Killing for Fun: Roman Bloodsport
and the "Spectacles"

THE UBIQUITOUS VIOLENCE OF the Roman society in which nascent
Christianity was incubated did not stop at the womb or the cradles
of infants. In the Coliseum and countless other venues across the empire,
people were slaughtered. . . . and the crowds roared their approval. These
were the infamous games, or as they were popularly known, "spectacles."[1]
The spectacles included such things as theatrical tragedies and comedies
about the foibles and exploits of the gods, chariot races, and fights to the
death in the gladiatorial arena. As we will come to see here, the teaching and discipline of the early church was just as strict against Christians
viewing or participating in the spectacles as it was against abortion, for
reasons that included both contempt for the inherent idolatry of the spectacles, and a profound aversion to the bloodshed that occurred there.

Minicius Felix provides us with another excellent entry point into
the discussion. The pagan character of the *Octavian* dialogue, named
Caecilius, accuses the Christians of the crime of abstention from some
of the most cherished rituals of Roman amusement and civic piety: "But
in the meantime, in your anxious state of expectation, you refrain from
honest pleasures: you do not go to our shows, you take no part in our pro-
cessions, you are not present at our public banquets, you shrink in horror
from our sacred games, from food ritually dedicated by our priests, from
drink hallowed by libation poured upon our altars. . . . (*Octavian* 12).
Caecilius's exasperated charges against the Christians, that they don't have
good, old-fashioned "fun," like watching gladiators butcher one another,
far from being a rhetorical exaggeration, is an accurate description of the

---

1. For an excellent introduction and overview of the Roman spectacles and blood-
sports, see Donald G. Kyle's *Spectacles of Death in Ancient Rome*.

61

Christian praxis of that era. The games were seen as simply idolatrous and evil. In a brief treatise on the Christian life to his friend Donatus, Cyprian, the third-century bishop of Carthage in northern Africa, offers a grim assessment of the state of a world in which horrific violence is considered pleasant entertainment:

> Now if you turn your eyes and face toward the cities themselves, you will find a multitude sadder than any solitude. A gladiatorial combat is being prepared that blood may delight the lust of cruel eyes. The body is filled up with stronger foods, and the robust mass of flesh grows fat with bulging muscles, so that fattened for pun-ishment it may perish more dearly. Man is killed for the pleasure of man, and to be able to kill is a skill, is an employment, is an art. Crime is not only committed but is taught. What can be called more inhuman, what more repulsive? It is a training that one may be able to kill, and that he kills is a glory. (*To Donatus* 7)

This same sense of horror and tragedy at the iniquities of the games is shared by other writers that era. Writing fifty years after Cyprian, Lactantius' disgust was at the fact that the Romans called these spectacles "games":

> For, although a man be condemned deservedly, whoever reck-ons it a pleasure for him to be strangled in his sight defiles his own conscience, just as surely as if he were a spectator and participant of a murder which is performed secretly. They call these games, however, in which human blood is spilled. So far has humanity departed from men that, when they kill the very life of men, they think that they are playing, but they are more harmful than all those whose blood they use for their pleasure. (*Divine Institutes* 6.20)

Note in Lactantius' words above how merely *witnessing* the murder of another human being (to say nothing of *participating* in it), whether publicly, as in the spectacles, or privately, "defiles one's conscience." Athenagoras was to take this a step further. Continuing his reply against the outlandish charge of cannibalism leveled against the Christians by suspicious pagans, he writes in his apology,

> Who can charge with murder or cannibalism men who are known to be unwilling to countenance even lawful homicide? Who is not held in thrall by armed contests and beast-fights, especially when they are sponsored by yourselves? But we consider the looking on

at a murder to be nigh to murder itself and forbid ourselves such spectacles. If then we do not even look on at these shows (so as not to be under a curse and to incur defilement), how can we be capable of murder? (*Embassy for Christians* 35)

Even *looking* at such a murder makes one complicit in murder, much as how looking lustfully at another's spouse makes one complicit in adultery. Because of this assumption, Christian bishops forbade their flocks from the abominable spectacles because of the moral stains that were imputed to the viewer.

So reprehensible were the spectacles to Tertullian that he composed an entire treatise on the subject. In it, he argues forcefully that faithful Christian disciples simply do not attend the Roman games because there is nothing redeeming in them whatsoever. In addition to the lines of argumentation laid out above, Tertullian attacks the origins of the games as idolatrous to their very core, for in addition to the bloodshed-as-sport which the Christians found detestable, the spectacles were always held in honor of some pagan deity, or else to celebrate the birthday of the divinized emperor. They usually involved sacrifices to the gods and tributes made in honor of and in appeasement to the dead. Thus Tertullian's comments concerning the bloody and sacrificial origins of the games:

For in time long past, in accordance with the belief that the souls of the dead are propitiated by human blood, they used to purchase captives or slaves of inferior ability and to sacrifice them at funerals. Afterwards, they preferred to disguise this ungodly usage by making it a pleasure. So after the persons thus procured had been trained- for the sole purpose of learning how to be killed!- in the use of such arms as they then had, and as best as they could wield, they then exposed them to death at the tombs on the day appointed for sacrifices in honor of the dead. Thus they found consolation for death in murder. Such is the origin of the gladiatorial contest. (*The Spectacles* 12.2–4)

As he continues his argument against the games, Tertullian then turns to the effect the games produce in those who view them. The chariot races and gladiator matches in particular, he says, are so defiling that "accordingly, from such beginnings the affair progresses to outbursts of fury and passion and discord and to everything forbidden to the priests of peace" (*The Spectacles* 16.4). Calling Christians the "priests of peace," Tertullian forcefully shows why their peaceful priesthood is defiled through the contagious and corrupting frenzy incited by the bloody games. Tatian, a second century disciple of Justin Martyr, also commenting on the degenerative effects the games have on those who view them, notes wryly how those fans of the games who happen to miss the climactic death blows are annoyed because they missed the gory "good stuff," much the same as fans of NASCAR auto racing are vexed if they happen to have missed seeing a spectacular car crash (*Address to the Greeks* 23.2). Above all else in the games however, it was the violence against the human person that the early Christians condemned: "But as for what is done in the stadium, you cannot deny that it is unfit for you to see—punches and kicks and blows and all the reckless use of the fist and every disfiguration of the human face, that is, of God's image" (Tertullian *The Spectacles* 18.1).

The church did not oppose all such "spectacles" however. The Christian who wanted to get his or her fix of entertainment was exhorted to seek out *God's* marvels and spectacles. The beauty of the sunset, the majesty of the ocean waves, the orderliness of the cycles of the moon and the other celestial bodies, the serenity of the skies and the clouds on a warm summer's day; in short, the contemplation of God in nature. *These* are the spectacles meant for consumption and appreciation by Christians, for they are far superior to any devised by human hands (Novatian the Presbyter, *The Spectacles*, 9).[2] To these, Tertullian added the holy works of Christians as spectacles to be appreciated. Instead of the literary accomplishments of the stage, depicting the exploits of Rome's mythological gods, "we have sufficient literature of our own, enough verses and maxims, also enough songs and melodies; and ours are not fables but truths, not artful devices, but plain realities" (Tertullian *The Spectacles* 29.4). Instead of the violent spectacles of boxing, wrestling, and gladiatorial contests, the Christian spectacles were of a different and superior quality altogether: "contests of no slight account, and plenty of them. Behold impurity overthrown by chastity, faithlessness slain by faith, cruelty crushed by mercy, impudence put in the shade by modesty. Such are the contests among us, and in these we win our crowns" (Tertullian *The Spectacles* 29.5). Likewise,

---

2. This treatise, long thought to have been spuriously attributed to Cyprian, is now widely recognized as the work of Cyprian's contemporary, Novatian the Presbyter. Novatian was a schismatic who set himself up as an antipope when he disputed the election of the bishop of Rome. His writings shepherded his church, which existed parallel to the Catholic church, for several centuries after his death. His treatise on the spectacles however, is modeled after Tertullian's treatment of the same subject fifty years before and is profitable for our survey of this subject here.

even those who felt the need for the blood of the spectacles would be have their needs met by the One who bled for them: "Do you have desire for blood too? You have the blood of Christ" (ibid.).

But the greatest spectacle of all has *already* been accomplished and could be beheld by all with eyes to see: "that devil who had triumphed over the whole world lying prostrate under the feet of Christ" (Novatian *The Spectacles* 10). Novatian continues in that same paragraph by marveling at the supreme spectacle of the devil, overpowered by the cross of Jesus Christ:

> How honourable is this exhibition, brethren! how delightful, how needful ever to gaze upon one's hope, and to open our eyes to one's salvation! *This* is a spectacle which is beheld even when sight is lost. *This* is an exhibition which is given by neither prætor nor consul, but by Him who is alone and above all things, and before all things, yea, and of whom are all things, the Father of our Lord Jesus Christ, to whom be glory and honour for ever and ever. (Ibid.)

9

Killing Ourselves: Suicide

T HE NEXT AREA OF concern for the church was a deep unease at the prospect of taking of one's own life- suicide. While there was no such word as *suicide* in any language in the ancient world,[1] the practice of voluntarily ending one's own life was as common in antiquity as it is today. Well-known to history are the suicides of Mark Antony, who fell upon his sword in true Roman fashion in 30 BCE and Cleopatra's suicide by poisonous snake shortly thereafter. There were also *forced* suicides, such as Socrates' death sentence for impiety and "corrupting youth" by drinking hemlock.[2]

The gossipy Roman historian Suetonius, in his *Lives of the Twelve Caesars*, tells of the end of the life of the despotic emperor Nero in 68 CE. Facing immanent revolt and betrayal on all sides after his descent in madness, Nero chose to end his own life in the classical way:

> The horsemen who had received orders to bring him away alive, were now approaching the house. As soon as he heard them coming, he uttered with a trembling voice the following verse, "The noise of swift-heel'd steeds assails my ears," he drove a dagger into his throat, being assisted in the act by Epaphroditus, his secretary. A centurion bursting in just as he was half-dead, and applying his cloak to the wound, pretending that he was come to his assistance, he made no other reply but this, "'Tis too late;" and "Is this your loyalty?" Immediately after pronouncing these words, he expired, with his eyes fixed and starting out of his head, to the terror of all who beheld him. He had requested of his attendants, as the most

1. Joyce Salisbury comments in *Blood of the Martyrs* that the word "suicide" was coined in the seventeenth century as a "perjorative condemnation of self-killing" (190).

2. The ancient sources are unanimous that Socrates could have avoided his death, as his followers were able to bribe the guards, but chose to remain because fleeing for fear of one's life was not considered a noble action of a true philosopher.

essential favour, that they would let no one have his head, but that by all means his body might be burnt entire.[3]

The crucial feature to observe here is Nero's concern for control over his own death. He wanted to be sure that he, rather than the conspirators plotting against him, determined the time, place, and manner of his death—even extending to how his body was to be treated after he killed himself. This concern for control over one's own death was commonplace in antiquity. "As Romans found themselves less able to exert control over their political lives during the empire, noble Romans cherished their continued ability to choose their own moment and means of death."[4] The act was a final measure of defiance toward one's enemies, an assertion of one's own honor and dignity in the face of scandal and accusations. It was a desperate assertion that even when all else was beyond your control, and the world seemed to be crumbling around you, you were still the boss of your own destiny.

Perhaps the most famous act of suicide in antiquity comes from the closing days of the Jewish War of 66–73 CE in a mountain fortress known as Masada in the Judean desert. As Roman siege engines relentlessly closed in and it became clear to the Jewish rebels holed up in the fortress that the end was near, they made a crucial decision; rather than die in battle or face the inevitable mass crucifixions that would occur if the Romans had taken them alive, they resolved to take their own lives. Josephus recounts in his *Jewish Wars* the impassioned speech by the leader of the rebels:

> While our hands are free and can hold a sword, let them do a noble service! Let us die unenslaved by our enemies, and leave this world as free men in company with our wives and children. That is what the Law ordains, that is what our wives and children demand of us, the necessity God has laid upon us, the opposite of what the Romans wish . . .[5]

And then, in a tragedy that continues to captivate our imaginations, the armed men killed their wives, children, and then one another, leaving the last man to die by his own hand. When the Romans finally breached the walls, they found only corpses, willingly slain by their own

---

3. Suetonius, *Life of Nero*, 49. Online: http://ancienthistory.about.com/library/bl/bl_nero_suetonius.htm.

4. Salisbury, *Blood of the Martyrs*, 190.

5. Cited in ibid., 192.

hands, rather than the bloody fight to the death they had anticipated. The rebels at Masada slaughtered themselves in an act of protest designed to rob the Romans of the pleasure of conquest, and to assert control over their own fate.

Suicide in antiquity then, usually took on the meaning of self-assertion and determining one's own destiny by taking one's own life. Christians however, rejected the notion that the individual has the right to take his or her own life. The prevailing concept we have observed of suicide as self-assertion and determination of one's own destiny was abhorrent to the Christians of antiquity because of their conviction that God alone has the right to take human life, for he gave it in the first place. Lactantius, arguing from the conviction that the intentional taking of the life of another human is always homicide, had this to say:

> For if homicide is wicked because it is a destroyer of a man, he who kills himself is fettered by the same guilt because he kills a man. In fact, this ought to be judged a greater crime, the punishment of which belongs to God alone. For, just as we came into this life not of our own accord, so departure from this domicile of the body which was assigned to our protection must be made at the order of the same One who put us into this body, to dwell therein until He should order us to leave. (*Divine Institutes* 3.18)

The underlying conviction here is that only the God who gave life may take it away again. Hence, those guilty of killing themselves are just as guilty of homicide as the common criminal who murders for selfish gain or the robber who kills for money. Later in that same passage, he even makes the countercultural argument that even those esteemed philosophers who took their own lives because of "honor" or "virtue" are in fact murderers, usurping the divine prerogative by taking human life (their own) which is not theirs to take in the first place.

Another consideration against suicide for the early church was the simple, pragmatic one of existence. The Christians were demonstrably eager to lay down their lives in a martyr's witness to the gospel, in imitation of the passion of Jesus (a fact to which I will return again toward the end of this book), and their pagan neighbors took notice of this. Evidently some began to taunt the Christians to the effect that "if you are so eager to get to your God, just kill yourselves so that we might be rid of you." Justin Martyr, in his *Second Apology* had a ready reply:

> But lest anyone say, "Go then all of you and commit suicide, and pass even now to God, and do not trouble us"—I will tell you why we do not do so, but how, when examined, we make our confession without fear. We have been taught that God did not make the world aimlessly, but for the sake of the human race; and we have stated before that He rejoices in those who imitate His nature, and is displeased with those who embrace what is worthless either in word or deed. (*Second Apology* 4)

That is to say, God created the world for a specific purpose—for the sake of humankind—and that those whom imitate God's nature (as revealed by his benevolent creation) are those who God favors. Justin says that God is *displeased*, however with those whose words or actions are worthless. This serves to flesh out his reasoning that if "we all commit suicide, we will become the cause, as far as in us lies, why no one should be born, or instructed in the divine teachings, or even why the human race should not exist; and if we so act, we ourselves will be acting in opposition to the will of God" (ibid.). Thus, those who take their lives are acting counter to the nature of God the creator. If all the Christians were to commit suicide as their pagan neighbors taunted them to do, the word of God would not be preached, and even the human race would cease to propagate, a fact which would entirely undermine the creative actions of God. The church bore witness that, in Justin's words, suicide is "acting in opposition to the will of God."

Origen was to state the matter even more categorically than either Lactantius or Justin: "No occasion for taking leave of life seems reasonable to us except that alone which is for the sake of piety or virtue, as when those who are supposed to be judges, or who seem to have power over our lives, offer us the alternative either to live and act contrary to the precepts enjoined by Jesus, or to die and believe his words" (*Against Celsus* 8.55). Christians have no acceptable occasion for deliberately taking leave of life, except the martyr's death in faithful obedience to Christ. In a social stance which was as countercultural as any the early church was to make, intentionally killing oneself for any reason runs contrary to God's will, usurps the divine prerogative, and turns one into a murderer.

But Origen's comments on martyrdom also open the way to a bit of a slippery slope. As we will see later, not only were many of the Christian martyrs willing to die as a witness to their faith in and allegiance to Jesus Christ, some of them were downright *eager* to die. The early church faced the widespread problem of Christians essentially volunteering for martyrdom—deliberately provoking the authorities into increasing the severity of their persecution, or stepping forward and proclaiming their Christian faith to the magistrates when none were asking. Origen himself, the legend has it, nearly met an early demise when in his youthful impetuousness, he was about to follow his father to a martyr's death when he was prevented from leaving his house when his mother hid his clothes. This eagerness to undergo the baptism of blood presented a problem for the church which prohibited suicide, and served to blur the line between suffering martyrdom and volunteering for martyrdom. Did those martyrs who stepped forward of their own accord during times of persecution commit suicide in doing so? The early church was uncomfortable with the notion of voluntary martyrdom in light of church teaching on suicide, and prohibited the practice, but the questions which this practice raised continue to plague our discussions of suicide to the present day.[6]

---

6. The discussion of the morality of suicide, and the question of just what constitutes suicide, is raised articulately in an article by Christine Gudorf, past president of the Society of Christian Ethics. See her "Heroes, Suicide, and Moral Discernment," 87–108.

10

Killing Our Enemies: War and Military Service

KILLING (NOT SOLDIERING) IS THE PROBLEM

WE TURN NOW TO the type of violence which the church has most readily embraced since the fourth century—killing in war. The old and venerable "just war" theory exhibits the care which later theologians would employ in attempt to bring church teaching to bear on the question of when it is right to kill another human being, but as we will see, before the Constantinian synthesis necessitated the development of "just war" notions, killing in war was *always* rejected as an acceptable option for Christians. On this question, the primary sources are in perfect accord.

However, conflicting literature has already been written on the contentious matter of the church's attitude(s) toward military service.[1] The issues are multifaceted and complicated, and I will not be able to address them exhaustively in this brief space. However, what I will do in this section to take the discussion in a hitherto lightly explored direction is to posit a thesis which I will attempt to show adequately accounts for the many apparently contradictory pieces of evidence and brings them into a coherent witness on the subject. *The church was not vehemently opposed to military service per se. Rather it was the specific activities of the soldier in the Roman legions which the church found to be incompatible with the gospel of Jesus Christ- idolatry and killing.* Instead of arguing over the presence of Christians in the Roman military and the church's attitude toward this, we ought to be considering military service as a subquestion under the heading of the church's attitude toward violence and bloodshed, for that was the real issue at stake, as I will demonstrate.

---

1. On the existing literature addressing this question and the wildly divergent conclusions these scholars have come to, see above, 52.

The centerpiece of my argument here is the *Apostolic Tradition*, usually associated with Hippolytus of Rome in the first decades of the third century.[2] The *Apostolic Tradition* is an example of a literary genre known as the "church order," which dictates various rules, regulations, and polities to be followed in the church as well as preserving the liturgical forms of certain prayers from the 3rd century and before. It is clearly an authoritative document, as numerous later church orders[3] were based on its framework and preserve large portions of its content intact. The basic text of the *Apostolic Tradition* "proceeded to give birth to almost all of the canonical Christian collections in many parts of the world," which establishes the fact that this document evinces "a kind of early Church consensus."[4] It was held to be authoritative for the church in many far-flung corners of the Roman Empire, where it was copied and recopied many times over.

This document's importance for our purposes comes in its clear addressing of the issues surrounding military service and violence. Chapter 16 is a lengthy list of requirements that individuals seeking baptism and membership in the church must meet, including close scrutiny of their professions. Some of those engaged in questionable professions are permitted to remain in their profession, so long as they modify their behavior to conform it to church discipline. For example, one who was a sculptor by trade was permitted to continue practicing his or her profession, provided that he or she did not craft idols for pagan customers. Others were required to quit their profession entirely, a category which included such objectionable professions as sorcerers and prostitutes. If the individual under scrutiny failed to meet the requirements for entry into the catechumenate or refused to quit or alter their profession as necessitated by the church order, they were simply rejected from catechumenal consideration and would never be permitted to receive baptism until their lives conformed to the rigorous church discipline.

2. The best edition of the *Apostolic Tradition* in print is that of Alistair Stewart-Sykes, from the *Popular Patristics* series published by St. Vladimir's Seminary Press in 2001. Stewart-Sykes holds that while the historical figure of Hippolytus may not have been directly responsible for the current text of the *Apostolic Tradition* as it stands, his school was critical in the document's development. He contends that contrary to some recent scholars, the *A.T.* must be regarded as Roman in origin, a fact which heightens its influence as a widely-followed church order.

3. Such as the *Apostolic Constitutions*, and the *Canons of Hippolytus*.

4. Hornus, *It Is Not Lawful for Me to Fight*, 161.

In this context, I lift up three canons in particular from chapter 16 which will serve as a key to unlocking the ambiguity that exists elsewhere in the patristic witness.

> (9.) A soldier in command must be told not to kill people; if he is ordered so to do, he shall not carry it out. Nor shall he take the oath. If he will not agree, he should be rejected [from the catechumenate]. (10.)Anyone who has the power of the sword, or who is a civil magistrate wearing the purple, should desist, or he should be rejected. (11.) If a catechumen or a believer wishes to become a soldier they should be rejected, for they have despised God. (*Apostolic Tradition* 16.9–11)

First in canon 9, the "soldier in command"[5] who seeks entry into the catechumenate in hopes of ultimate baptism is included among those who must modify their behavior before acceptance. The soldier who wants to become a Christian must refuse to kill anyone, even if ordered to do so; likewise he shall not take the (idolatrous) military oath. Violating either of these two conditions would mean automatic exclusion or expulsion from the catechumenate. Yet it is significant to note that the soldier is not explicitly ordered to quit soldiering. For many soldiers, quitting the army before their term of service had expired would have entailed an almost certain death sentence. This is an extension of grace from the church to those soldiers who had been evangelized as the gospel message penetrated deeper into the Roman Empire. Those who were already soldiers at the time of their conversion could stay in their posts as long as they did not swear the military oath or, more importantly for our purposes here, kill anyone.

The next canon speaks to those who are higher up in the chain of military authority. Those with "the power of the sword" (military officials) or "civil magistrates wearing the purple" (a symbol of the authority of the Empire), are not extended the same grace which is given to lower-ranking soldiers. They are told in no uncertain terms that if they wish to join the church, they must resign their posts or else face rejection from the catechumenate. Was it service to the empire which was in and of itself objectionable? The phrasing that anyone who has "the power of the sword" must quit strongly suggests otherwise. In fact, the sword *itself* was

---

5. Stewart-Sykes is emphatic in his commentary on this passage that despite the "in command" the context makes clear that what is referred to here is not a commander, but a soldier of inferior rank, a lowly grunt, or private in today's terminology.

the cause of the objection in this case. This was something fundamentally incompatible with the gospel of life which gave the church its significant moral scruples in this area.

The third and final canon from the *Apostolic Tradition* that bears scrutiny for our purposes tells us that the catechumen or believer (i.e., full, baptized member of the church) who wishes to *become* a soldier must be rejected, "for they have despised God." This canon is not addressing those who are already soldiers, as was canon 9, but those within the church (or desirous of being in the church) who also wish to become soldiers in Caesar's legions. The answer the church gave to this desire is an unambiguous "No."

In sum, according to the *Apostolic Tradition*, soldiers who seek to become Christians may for pragmatic reasons remain in their current occupation provided they do not kill anyone. However Christians or catechumens who seek to take up a profession of arms are forbidden from doing so, under penalty of excommunication. The tolerance of converts who were already in the army strongly indicates that it was not military service as such to which the church objected, but it was the killing which is so frequently inherent in the occupation of a soldier that was unacceptable to church discipline. Hornus sums up the evidence well when he says that chapter 16 of the *Apostolic Tradition* "proves that the Church expressed itself officially on this subject, and that it clearly condemned in the army the homicidal violence which is its fundamental characteristic."[6] We should keep these fundamental points from this church consensus document in mind as we move forward. I will be using them as an interpretive lens through which to view the other evidence from this period concerning the church and the military.

Further demonstrating that it was the bloodshed of military life to which the early church objected are the many and multifaceted condemnations of war found throughout the literature of the Fathers. The warlike Romans, who felt compelled as benevolent conquerors (as they saw themselves) to maintain a sort of "peace"[7] through overwhelming force of arms, felt strongly that Rome's greatness and strength were due to her citizens' piety in their devotion to civic religion, and the practice of virtue, through the esteem in which they held the philosophers. Minicius Felix's

6. Hornus, 161.

7. For an excellent analysis and discussion of the *Pax Romana*, see Klaus Wengst's *Pax Romana and the Peace of Jesus Christ*.

character Octavius turns the Romans' self-congratulatory rhetoric of piety and virtue on its head, pointing out the real reason for Rome's dominance in the ancient world: "The consequence is that whatever the Romans hold, occupy, and possess is the booty of outrage. All their temples come from the plunder of war, and that means the destruction of cities, the pillaging of gods, the slaughter of priests." It was Roman ruthlessness and bloodshed on a massive scale which held the *Pax Romana*. "It follows that Rome is so great not because she has been devoutly religious but because she has been sacrilegious and gone unpunished" (*Octavian* 25). Tatian, writing a few decades before Minicius Felix, observed the brutality of Roman society (even its most upstanding citizens), and used it as an argument against the prevailing notion that immutable fate determined the outcome of everything: "How then can I accept the doctrine of fate-ordained nativity when I see that its ministers are like *this*?" The following statement makes clear both his indignation with the bloody state of affairs in Rome, but also exhibits how Christians of his day did not want anything to do with wealth, power, or the military: "I have no desire to rule, I do not wish to be rich; I do not seek [military] command" (*Address to the Greeks* 11.1). This disdain for military command showcases the theological attitude prevailing among the early Christians. Knowledge of the one true God, it was supposed, would lead to a complete rejection of warfare and its pointless slaughter; hence the violence of those who did not yet know God: "Because you do not know God you make war among yourselves and kill one another . . ." (Tatian *Address to the Greeks* 26.3).

Clement of Alexandria, in his exposition of Christ as an educator, argues that the lives of Christians were better and more useful than those of the pagans because the simple lives Christians lived did not require extensive equipment or material possessions. This is especially true in the realm of war: "We are educated not for war, but for peace," he argued. "In war, there is need for much equipment, just as self-indulgence craves an abundance. But peace and love, simple and plain blood sisters, do not need arms nor abundant supplies. Their nourishment is the Word, the Word whose leadership enlightens and educates, from whom we learn poverty and humility and all that goes with love of freedom and of mankind and of the good. In a word, through Him, we become like God by a likeness of virtue" (*Christ the Educator* 1.12). In another place, Clement was discussing the virtues of Christian women as contrasted with their pagan counterparts. Noting the warlike nature of the famous Amazon women, he writes: "For we do not train our women like Amazons to manliness in war; since we wish the men even to be peaceable" (*Stromata* 4.8). How can Christian women be trained for war when even Christian men are not?

Clement's fellow Alexandrian and eventual successor as head of the Alexandrian catechetical school, Origen, also comments on Christian attitudes toward war in general. The pagan philosopher Celsus had alleged that Christianity had its historical origins in a violent "revolt against the community," to which Origen responded,

> If a revolt had been the cause of the Christians existing as a separate group (and they originated from the Jews for whom it was lawful to take up arms in defense of their families and to serve in wars), the lawgiver of the Christians would not have forbidden entirely the taking of human life. He taught that it was never right for his disciples to go so far against a man, even if he should be very wicked; for he did not consider it compatible with his inspired legislation to allow the taking of human life in any form at all. (*Against Celsus* 3.7)

Origen makes two essential points in his rebuttal to Celsus which will arise again elsewhere frequently. First, he makes a clear distinction between Christians and Jews, "for whom it was lawful to take up arms in defense of their families and to serve in wars." This suggests a view of progressive revelation that, while God had permitted warfare under the Old Covenant, under the New such permission has been revoked.[8] Second, the Christian Lawgiver (Christ) had "forbidden entirely the taking of human life," and whose inspired legislation did not "allow the taking of human life in any form at all." For Origen, the fact that Christians are prohibited from killing other human beings under any circumstances is more than enough to refute Celsus' baseless accusation.

The issue of Christian participation in military service rises even more directly later on in Origen's reply to Celsus. Celsus, Origen reports, exhorted Christians to "help the emperor with all our power, and cooperation with him in what is right, and fight for him, and be fellow-soldiers if he presses for this, and fellow-generals with him" (*Against Celsus* 8.73).

---

8. This observation helps explain Clement of Alexandria's often cited praise of Moses' skill as a military commander in *Stromateis* 1.24. Clement, like Origen, recognized that the Jews living under the Old Covenant had no such prohibition of warfare (as the Christians living under the New Covenant did), and indeed were even commanded to it by God.

Implicit in Celsus' charge is the assumption that Christians of his day *do not* fight in wars for the emperor, an assumption Origen himself confirms for us later in the chapter. Celsus' charge here was essentially one of civic irresponsibility—that the Christians were not doing their duty as Roman citizens, a duty which would have included fighting in the imperial legions. Origen's reply to this point is both extraordinarily creative, and illustrative of what we observe elsewhere in the patristic literature.

> We may reply to this that at appropriate times we render to the emperors divine help, if I may so say, by taking up even the whole armour of God. And this we do in obedience to the apostolic utterance which says: "I exhort you, therefore, first to make prayers, supplications, intercessions, and thanksgivings for all men, for emperors and all that are in authority." Indeed, the more pious a man is, the more effective his is in helping the emperors—more so than soldiers who go out into the lines and kill all the enemy troops that they can . . . (*Against Celsus* 8.74)

Origen replies to this charge of civic irresponsibility by arguing that through their prayers, Christians are actually *more* efficacious and helpful to the emperor than are those who kill scores of enemy soldiers. In effect, because of their obedience to the biblical injunctions to pray for those in power, the Christians serve the emperor better than do those who kill in the emperor's name. Origen's profound faith in the power of prayer is evident here. He continues:

> Moreover, we who by our prayers destroy all daemons which stir up wars, violate oaths, and disturb the peace, are of more help to the emperors than those who seem to be doing the fighting. We who offer prayers with righteousness, together with ascetic practices and exercises which teach us to despise pleasures and not to be led by them, are cooperating in the tasks of the community. Even more do we fight on behalf of the emperor. And though we do not become fellow-soldiers with him, even if he presses for this, yet we are fighting for him and composing a special army of piety through our intercessions to God. (*Against Celsus* 8.74)

Christian "prayer warriors" are, in truth, the emperor's best friends, for although they do not serve in his armies and kill for him, by their prayers, they compose "a special army of piety" which is far greater and more efficacious than the death-dealing exploits of the imperial legions.

THE CHURCH AS "AN ARMY THAT SHEDS NO BLOOD": THE MILITIA CHRISTI AND THE MILITIA ROMANA

This leads us directly into another point which is essential for a proper understanding of the early Christians' attitude toward the military—the imagery of the *militia Christi*.[9] Ancient Christian literature is replete with militaristic imagery and metaphors, which is curious considering the church's ambivalence toward the Roman military machine. The church is continually likened to an army, but an army unlike any the world has ever seen. Here, I'll lift up some examples of *militia Christi* imagery in the patristic literature to give a flavor of the militaristic language, and then offer a few comments by way of analysis.

Military metaphors appear in some of the earliest noncanonical Christian literature. Clement of Rome, writing at the end of the first century, writes to reconcile the schismatic Corinthian church and to exhort the Christians there to unity, discipline, and peace with one another. Taking the well-known model of the fiercely disciplined Roman army as the model of obedience to church leaders he wishes the Corinthians would emulate, he writes,

> Let us then, brethren, do soldier's duty in downright earnest under the banner of His glorious commands. Let us observe those who are soldiering under our commanders, and see how punctually, how willingly, how submissively they execute the commands! Not all are prefects, or tribunes, or centurions, or lieutenants, and so on; but each in his own rank executes the orders of the emperor and the commanders. (*1 Clement* 37)

The analogy here is clear—"our commanders" are the bishops and presbyters. Clement is exhorting the church to obedience to their "commanders," in contrast to the factiousness and dissention then plaguing the church at Corinth. While Clement may be taking his inspiration from the legendary discipline of the Roman legions, this must not be misconstrued, as some have,[10] as Clement approving of the military vocation, to say nothing of the murderous violence of the legions. Lactantius declared that the worship of God "is a kind of heavenly military service" (*Divine*

9. I.e., "Christian military." This phrase was made famous by Adolph von Harnack's now-classic study of the early church and war, *Militia Christi*.

10. E.g., Alexander F. C. Webster, "Justifiable war as a 'lesser good' in Eastern Orthodox theology." *St. Vladimir's Theological Quarterly* 47 (2003) 3–57.

Institutes 5.19), while even the paradigmatic pacifist Tertullian called the church "God's militia" (*On Prayer* 19.5). Elsewhere, Tertullian exhorted the martyrs to faithfulness using similar militaristic metaphors: "Grant now, O blessed, that even to Christians the prison is unpleasant- yet we were called to the service in the army of the living God in the very moment when we gave response to the words of the sacramental oath" (*To the Martyrs* 3.1). The "sacramental oath" (*sacramentum* in Latin) was the oath soldiers gave when joining the Roman army, swearing allegiance to the emperor and to the gods. Tertullian uses it here to refer to the baptismal vows, swearing allegiance to God, thus robbing the word of its force for the secular, military world. And in his *Apology*, with more than a little twist of irony and humor considering the Christian church's stance against violence, he writes, "We come together for a meeting and a congregation, in order to besiege God with prayers, like an army in battle formation. Such violence is pleasing to God" (*Apology* 39.2).

One unique facet about this military imagery is the early church's insistence that despite the fact that Christians were an "army" of sorts, they did not shed blood as the armies of the world did nor wield worldly weapons (2 Cor 10:3–5). Clement of Alexandria is typical of this pattern. First, from his *Exhortation to the Greeks*:

> But when the shrilling trumpet blows, it assembles the soldiers and proclaims war; and shall not Christ, think you, having breathed to the ends of the earth a song of peace, assemble the soldiers of peace that are his? Yes, and He did assemble, O man, by blood and by word His bloodless army, and to them He entrusted the kingdom of heaven. The trumpet of Christ is his gospel. He sounded it, and we heard. Let us gird ourselves with the armour of peace, "putting on the breastplate of righteousness," and taking up the shield of faith and placing on our head the helmet of salvation; and let us sharpen "the sword of the spirit, which is the word of God." Thus does the apostle marshal us in the ranks of peace. (*Exhortation to the Greeks* 11)

In this powerful passage, Clement calls Christians "soldiers of peace" and Christ's "bloodless army," leaving no doubt as to what sort of militia the Christians comprise. Also of note here is the allusion to one of the military metaphor passages of the New Testament, Ephesians 6:10–18, which, Clement notes, "marshal[s] us in the ranks of peace." In another place, Clement makes much the same point:

> Do not you be deceived, however, who have tasted of truth, and
> have been deemed worthy of the great redemption; but contrary
> to the rest of men, enlist on your behalf an army without weapons,
> without war, without bloodshed, without anger, without stain, an
> army of God-fearing old men, of God-beloved orphans, of wid-
> ows armed with gentleness, of men adorned with love. Obtain with
> your wealth, as guards for your body and your soul, such men as
> these, whose commander is God. Through them the sinking ship
> rises, steered by the prayers of saints alone; and sickness at its
> height is subdued, put to flight by the laying on of hands; the at-
> tack of robbers is made harmless, being stripped of its weapons by
> pious prayers; and the violence of daemons is shattered, reduced
> to impotence by confident commands. (*Who is the Rich Man That
> Is Being Saved?* 34)

Comprising "an army without weapons, without war, without bloodshed," the Christians fight against the demonic darkness and human evil
with their weapons of pious prayer, the laying on of hands, and exorcisms.
These passages serve to underscore my thesis—that it was not so much
military service to which the church objected as it was the bloodshed of
the armies of the world. For the early Christians, the church *is* an army;
albeit one that sheds no blood.

As the Christians were likened to an army, so was martyrdom and
public confession of the faith likened to the warfare proper for Christians.
Cyprian of Carthage, often wont to employ military metaphors himself,
served as a model of this Christian "combat" when he made his public
confession of faith and held out under physical torture rather than deny
Christ. In a letter commending Cyprian for his faithful witness and model
for Christians everywhere, a group of imprisoned clergy praises Cyprian
for his exemplary spiritual warfare:

> With that trumpet call you roused the soldiers of God whom you
> have now furnished with heavenly weapons to engage in the en-
> counter, and in the front line of battle you slew the devil yourself
> with your spiritual sword. With those words of yours you arrayed
> in due order, on this side and that, the battle lines of your brethren.
> The foe was thus beset with snares on every side, his sinews were
> severed, and the very carcass of our common enemy was trampled
> underfoot. (Cyprian *Epistle 77*)

Origen furnishes another example. Writing to a group of his
friends, imprisoned for their profession of faith, Origen exhorts them

to the spiritual combat of martyrdom: "A great multitude is assembled to watch you when you combat and are called to martyrdom . . . all will hear you fighting the fight for Christianity" (*Exhortation to Martyrdom* 18). The deaths of Origen's friends will be witnessed by a great multitude as a public spectacle. What better opportunity to bear witness to their steadfast faith and the Lord's great love? He employs combat metaphors to describe martyrdom, the shedding of their *own* blood rather than the blood of others.

The Christians' strong convictions against participation in warfare even influenced their interpretation of the Old Testament passages which narrate the wars of Yahweh. In his spiritualized exegesis of Joshua, one of the bloodiest books of the Old Testament, Origen finds himself compelled to read the Old Testament as allegorical rather than historical: "Unless those carnal wars [i.e., of the Old Testament] were a symbol of spiritual wars, I do not think that the Jewish historical books would ever have been passed down by the Apostles to be read by Christ's followers in their churches" (*Homilies on Joshua* 16:1). Even though we modern readers may find his spiritualized exegesis strained at this point, one must admire Origen's attempt to wrestle honestly with a passage which presented problems for his nonviolent convictions. His conclusion leaves no doubt on where he stands with regard to the question of Christians and warfare: "Thus, the Apostle, being aware *that physical wars are no longer to be waged by us* but that our struggles are to be only battles of the soul against spiritual adversaries, gives orders to the soldiers of Christ like a military commander when he says, 'Put on the armor of God so as to be able to hold your ground against the wiles of the devil'" (my emphasis).

The Marcionite heresy was the first widespread internal crisis the church was to face in its struggle to define orthodoxy. Marcion and his followers contrasted what they saw as the violent, vengeful Creator God of the Old Testament with the kind and loving Father revealed in the New Testament, and concluded that they simply must be different gods. To build his case, Marcion compiled a book of *Antitheses*, contrasting violent quotations from the Old Testament with irenic citations from the New. Among his Old Testament citations were messianic prophecies from Isaiah, which Marcion believed showed that the Christ promised in the Old Testament was to be a mighty and powerful warrior. Tertullian, in his five-volume response to Marcion's assertions, challenged that reading, and presented evidence to show that the Old Testament prophecies of the

Messiah actually foretold a gentle and peaceful ruler, not a warlike tyrant. He challenges Marcion on his reading: "Come now, you who suppose the prophecy [of Christ] was of a militant and armed warrior, not as a figure or an allegory of one who on a spiritual battlefield, with spiritual armour, was to wage spiritual war against spiritual enemies" (*Against Marcion* 4.20). Similar to Origen's take on the Old Testament wars, Tertullian adopts a spiritualized Old Testament exegesis of the messianic prophecies in order to show that they actually applied to Jesus, not to some warrior-messianic figure. Marcion's strained exegesis, Terullian says, misses sight of the peaceful Messiah who does not wage war as the world does, but fights spiritual battles against the demonic forces. Commenting on Eph 4:8,

> "He led captivity captive," the apostle says. With what armour? in what battles? by laying waste what nation? by overthrowing what city? what women, what children, what chieftains, has this conqueror put in chains? For when in David Christ is prophesied of as girded with a sword upon his thigh, or in Isaiah as receiving the spoils of Samaria and the riches of Damascus, you force him to become truly and visibly a warrior. Observe then here is spiritual armoury and warfare ... (*Against Marcion* 5.18.)

The *militia Christi* imagery is so pervasive in the early church literature that the casual reader who is not fully aware of the context may mistake it for *actual* militarism. This is a terrible misreading of the martial metaphors in the patristic documents. Sadly, it's also a common one. For example, G. W. Clarke, the editor and translator of Cyprian's letters in the *Ancient Christian Writers* series, falls into this trap when he comments that "Cyprian's spiritual militancy, his lavish and elaborate employment of military imagery and metaphor in the glorification of martyrdom, is not suggestive of a notably pacifist mentality."[11] This is a gross misunderstanding, particularly considering the many quotes we have already seen about how the Christian army, the *militia Christi*, does not shed human blood. The *militia Christi* must not be misconstrued to be *actual* militancy, nor may it be seen as indicative of the Christians' attitude toward the Roman legions.[12] Rather, it seems more illustrative of my hypothesis that

11. 2:192 n. 15.

12. In truth, the most illustrative quote about the Roman army comes from Ignatius of Antioch, whose experiences with Roman soldiers while traveling to his martyrdom compelled him to write: "All the way from Syria to Rome I am fighting wild beasts, on

the church did not reject military service *as such*, but only the military's inherent bloodshed and idolatry. Indeed, they were happy to be part of an army—albeit a spiritual army that shed no blood!

The one major exception to this is Tertullian. Later in his life, Tertullian became so disgusted with the Roman legions, that he felt the church's position (which tolerated converted soldiers remaining in the army, provided they did not kill anyone—see above concerning the *Apostolic Tradition*), was too lax. Ever the moral rigorist, Tertullian's work contains two forceful passages that blast even *remaining* in the military as an acceptable option for converted soldiers, a step beyond official church teaching which only prohibited human bloodshed. First, in *On the Military Crown*, Tertullian responded to a pastoral crisis in which a recently converted Roman soldier threw down his military equipment in front of his commanders in a public display of defiance and witness. While more cautious voices in the church counseled patience and prudence, Tertullian exhorted all converted soldiers who remained in the army to follow their brother's example and quit as a public witness to where their true obedience lay. Then in a long series of biting rhetorical questions, he asks whether military service is at all compatible with the life of Christian discipleship:

> Now, to come down to the very heart of this question about the soldier's crown, should we not really first examine the right of a Christian to be in the military service at all? In other words, why discuss the merely accidental detail, when the foundation on which it rests is deserving of censure? Are we to believe it lawful to take an oath of allegiance to a mere human being over and above the oath of fidelity to God? Can we obey another master, having chosen Christ? Can we forsake father, mother, and all our relatives? By divine law we must honor them and our love for them is second only to that which we have toward God. The Gospel also bids us honor our parents, placing none but Christ Himself above them. Is it likely we are permitted to carry a sword when our Lord said that he who takes the sword will perish by the sword? Will the son of peace who is forbidden to engage in a lawsuit espouse the deeds of war? Will a Christian, taught to turn the other cheek when struck unjustly, guard prisoners in chains, and administer torture and capital punishment? Will he rather mount guard for

land and sea, chained as I am to ten leopards, that is, a detachment of soldiers, who prove themselves the more malevolent for kindness shown them. . . ." (Ignatius *Romans* 5).

> others than for Christ on station days [i.e., fast days]? And what
> about the Lord's Day? Will he not even then do it for Christ? Will
> he stand guard before temples, that he has renounced? Will he eat
> at pagan banquets, which the Apostle forbids? Will he protect by
> night those very demons whom in the daytime he has put to flight
> by his exorcisms, leaning on a lance such as pierced the side of
> Christ? Will he bear, too, a standard that is hostile to Christ, and
> will he ask the watch-word from his commander-in-chief—he
> who has already received one from God? (*On the Military Crown*
> 11.1–3)

In Tertullian's mindset, the very nature of military service, every
activity performed by a soldier of ancient Rome, was idolatrous and im-
moral. Especially marked out is the carrying (and ostensibly, the use) of a
sword—for "our Lord said that he who takes the sword will perish by the
sword" (an allusion to Matt 26:52). Likewise, Christians, here called "sons
of peace,"[13] by virtue of their obedience to the Sermon on the Mount,
simply cannot participate in the "deeds of war" and other activities naturally part of the soldier's life. For a Christian to become a soldier was little
more than an act of betrayal to Christ: "Yes, there and many other offenses
can be observed in the discharge of military duties- offenses that must be
interpreted as acts of desertion. To leave the camp of Light and enlist in
the camp of Darkness means going over to the enemy" (*On the Military
Crown* 11.4). Then in a nod to the official church teaching that those
who converted to Christianity while in the army should be permitted to
stay in their positions as long as their behavior conforms to the gospel
standards, Tertullian acknowledges "To be sure, the case is different for
those who are converted after they have been bound to military service.
St. John admitted soldiers to baptism; then there were the two most faithful centurions: the one whom Christ praised, and the other whom Peter
instructed." But here, he launches his scathing criticism of what he saw as
the moral laxity of the church's teaching: "But, once we have embraced the
faith and have been baptized, we either must immediately leave military
service (as many have done); or we must resort to all kinds of excuses
in order to avoid any action which is also forbidden in civilian life, lest
we offend God" (*On the Military Crown* 11.4). "What good is a soldier
who does not kill?" Tertullian reasons. It is better that Christian soldiers

---

13. Recall that elsewhere, Tertullian has called Christians "priests of peace" (*The
Spectacles*, 16) in addition to the nomenclature "sons of peace" here.

should simply quit, rather than tiptoeing around the forbidden conduct of killing and idolatry.

In his treatise *On Idolatry*, Tertullian again explicitly takes up the question of military service by Christians. This passage begins very similarly to his treatment of the subject in *On the Military Crown*, with comparisons between the duties of soldiers and Way of Jesus, and a declaration that a Christian's loyalty may be given to one master:

> But now inquiry is made about this point, whether a believer may turn himself unto military service, and whether the military may be admitted unto the faith, even the rank and file, or each inferior grade, to whom there is no necessity for taking part in sacrifices or capital punishments. There is no agreement between the divine and the human sacrament, the standard of Christ and the standard of the devil, the camp of light and the camp of darkness. One soul cannot be due to two masters—God and Caesar. (*On Idolatry* 19)

Tertullian then shows evidence of his hermeneutical sophistication. Recognizing the military attire and even participation in war by God's people from before Christ's Incarnation, Tertullian admits all this, and yet still insists on the normativity of nonviolence as taught by Jesus:

> And yet Moses carried a rod, and Aaron wore a buckle, and John (Baptist) is girt with leather and Joshua the son of Nun leads a line of march; and the People warred: if it pleases you to sport with the subject. But how will a Christian man war, nay, how will he serve even in peace, without a sword, which the Lord has taken away? For albeit soldiers had come unto John, and had received the formula of their rule; albeit, likewise, a centurion had believed; still the Lord afterward, in disarming Peter, unbelted every soldier. (*On Idolatry* 19)

He interprets Jesus' disarming Peter in the garden as an act of disarmament of all Christian soldiers, who should not, in his judgment, serve in the military, even in peacetime, because the Lord "has taken away" the sword from his disciples. Tertullian, like the rest of the early church, made a distinction between the ethics of Christians (who were forbidden from killing by their Lord), and the ethics of the Jews, who had not yet had the cruciform ethic of nonviolence revealed to them.

THE SWORD OR THE GOSPEL:
CHRISTIAN SOLDIER-MARTYRS

No survey of early Christians in the Roman military would be complete without an analysis of the soldier-martyrs recorded in the church's martyrology. Herbert Musurillo's definitive collection of *The Acts of the Christian Martyrs* contains five accounts of soldiers who were "outted" as Christians, some by their own initiative, as the soldier in Tertullian's *On the Military Crown*, some by others. Each one of them however witnessed for his faith in the face of persecution, and each died a martyr's death. Here, I will briefly analyze these five accounts, with an eye to hearing in the martyr's own words his attitude toward military service, and particularly toward violence.

First, the case of Marinus. Marinus was a soldier who had apparently been in the ranks for some time, as he was next in line for promotion to centurion when a post fell vacant. Before he could be promoted however, he was denounced to the magistrate as a Christian by a jealous rival. The magistrate demanded Marinus reconsider his Christian faith, and gave him a three hour window to think it over. What happened next is demonstrative of the church's attitude:

> No sooner had Marinus left the court than Theotecnus, the bishop of Caesarea, approached and drew him aside in conversation; taking him by the hand he led him to the church. Once inside, he placed Marinus' right hand in front of the altar, and drawing aside Marinus' cloak pointed to the sword attached to his side. At the same time, he brought a copy of the divine Gospels and he set it before Marinus, asking him to choose which he preferred. Without hesitation, Marinus put out his hand and took the divine writings. "So then," said Theotecnus, "hold fast to God, and given strength by him, may you obtain what you have chosen. Now go in peace." (*The Martyrdom of St. Marinus*, cited in Musurillo)

In his hour of decision, Marinus was challenged by the local bishop-either follow the gospels, or continue the life of the sword. Marinus chose the former, was commended to God by the bishop, and subsequently lost his head at the hands of the magistrate. This story illustrates the concrete, visceral choice as the early church saw it between following God's way, and continuing in the way of the world as epitomized by the sword's violence.

The story of Marcellus, another soldier-martyr, narrates the story of a centurion who "outed" himself willingly, and unlike Marinus, through no coercion by others. At a festival celebrating the birthday of the emperor,

> a centurion named Marcellus rejected these pagan festivities, and after throwing down his soldier's belt in front of the legionary standards which were there at the time, he bore witness in a loud voice: "I am a soldier of Jesus Christ, the eternal king. From now on I cease to serve your emperors and I despise the worship of your gods of wood and stone, for they are deaf and dumb images."
> (*The Acts of Marcellus* 1, Recension M, cited in Musurillo)

No indication whatsoever is given as to what prompted Marcellus to do this. As demonstrated by his rank, Marcellus must have been a soldier for quite some time, though we are given no clues as to when he had became a Christian. Perhaps he was following the injunctions of Tertullian, or perhaps he had only recently worked out the implications of his faith for his profession and took this public opportunity to witness to his faith as he threw down his arms. In any event, the conversation which follows stresses Marcellus' now firm belief in the incompatibility of the military life with the vocation of Christian discipleship:

> Agricolanus [the praetorian prefect] said: "Did you say the things that are recorded in the prefect's report?"
> "Yes, I did," answered Marcellus.
> "You held the military rank of centurion, first class?" asked Agricolanus.
> "Yes," said Marcellus.
> "What madness possessed you," asked Agricolanus, "to throw down the symbols of your military oath and to say the things you did?"
> Marcellus replied, "No madness possesses those who fear the Lord."
> "Then you did say all of these things," asked Agricolanus, "that are set down in the prefect's report?"
> "Yes, I said them," answered Marcellus.
> Agricolanus said: "You threw down your weapons?"
> Marcellus replied: "Yes, I did. For it is not fitting that a Christian, who fights for Christ his Lord, should fight for the armies of this world." (*Acts of Marcellus* 4)

In Marcellus' final comment, the *militia Christi* imagery returns with force. In his view, a Christian who "fights" for Christ simply cannot fight (literally) for worldly armies.[14]

While Marinus was outed as a Christian unwillingly, and Marcellus identified himself as such by his own initiative, the passion of Maximilian of Tebessa recounts the story of a young Christian who refused to join the Roman legions, even when forced to do so under compulsion. In the three short chapters that record Maximilian's conversation with the proconsul Dion, he repeatedly refuses to serve on the grounds that "I am a Christian!" a justification he declares no fewer than five times in the brief conversation. This excerpt provides a glimpse of the flavor and tone of the account:

> The proconsul Dion said: "What is your name?"
> Maximilian replied: "But why do you wish to know my name? I cannot serve [*militare*] because I am a Christian."
> The proconsul Dion said: "Get him ready."
> While he was being made ready, Maximilian replied: "I cannot serve. I cannot commit a sin. I am a Christian."
> "Let him be measured," said the proconsul Dion.
> After he was measured, one of the staff said: "He is five foot ten."
> Dion said to his staff: "Let him be given the military seal."
> Still resisting, Maximilian replied: "I will not do it! I cannot serve!" (*The Acts of Maximilian* 1, cited in Musurillo)

Maximilian's adamant refusal to violate his conscience and his faith by joining the Roman legions is best explained by the widespread adherence among the early church to the teaching of the *Apostolic Tradition* on this matter. Recall that canon 16.11 says that any Christians or catechumens who seek to become a soldier must be rejected, "for they have despised God." Maximilian's story is indicative of the deeply-ingrained antimilitaristic attitude which was inculcated in youth raised as Christians in the 3rd century. And as if to demonstrate that Maximilian's attitude was not out of sync with mainstream Christian thought and praxis, the hagiographer ends this account with a mention that after Maximilian's death, he was buried on a hill in Carthage, next to the body of Cyprian,

---

14. So forceful is this sentiment that even the non-pacifist reader, such as Alexander F. C. Webster, is forced to admit that Marcellus' remark "possesses the full force of absolute pacifism" (*Pacifist Option*, 187).

the greatest bishop-confessor-martyr and champion of orthodoxy in the mid 3rd century, a step which strongly implies approval and honoring of Maximilian's actions.

The story of Dasius is similar to that of Marinus, in that Dasius too was "outed" as a Christian by others. Dasius was a low-ranking soldier who had been selected by lot to play the part of the god Saturn in the customary feast and pageantry devoted to the Roman deity. Needless to say, Dasius objected vociferously, and made it known that he could not do this, for he was a Christian. To this point, ethical scruples about violence don't seem to play much part in the narrative, but when threatened with death by Bassus the commander unless he complied, Dasius' reply cuts straight to the heart of the early Christian objections to military service: "I have already told you and I repeat, I am a Christian, and I do not fight for any earthly king but for the king of heaven. His is the bounty I possess, I live by his favour, and I am wealthy because of his ineffable kindness" (*The Martyrdom of the Saintly Dasius*, cited in Musurillo). Dasius would not "not fight for any earthly king but for the king of heaven." Even though he remained in the army after his conversion, Dasius seems to have done so only in name only, refusing to participate in the idolatrous festival of Saturn, and refusing the fighting and violence of earthly soldiers. This, coupled with the *militia Christi* imagery, shows that even here, the polity represented by the *Apostolic Tradition* remained in force as church discipline.

The final account of a soldier martyr is that of Julius the Veteran. This is the one martyrdom account in which a Christian is said to have fought and been valiant in battle—seemingly implying killing. But all is not as it appears. Julius had been exposed under Diocletian's purge of Christians from the army, ordered to sacrifice, but he refused. Here is the relevant portion of the story, picking up where Julius was asked to offer a sacrifice:

> The prefect Maximus said: "What is so serious about offering some incense and going away?"
>
> Julius replied: "I cannot despise the divine commandments or appear unfaithful to my God. In all the twenty-seven years in which I made the mistake [*errare*], so it appears, to serve foolishly in the army, I was never brought before a magistrate either as a criminal or a trouble-maker. I went on seven military campaigns, and never hid behind anyone nor was I the inferior of any man in

battle. My chief never found me at fault. And now do you suppose that I, who was always found to be faithful in the past, should now be unfaithful to higher orders?"

"What military service did you have?" asked Maximus the prefect.

"I was in the army," answered Julius, "and when I had served my term I re-enlisted as a veteran. All of this time I worshipped in fear the God who made heaven and earth, and even to this day I show him my service." (*The Martyrdom of Julius the Veteran*, cited in Musurillo)

The first thing to note in this account is that Julius had been a soldier for twenty-seven years, and had served valiantly in battle—actual physical battle, not just *militia Christi* metaphorical or spiritual battle. If we take what he says here at face value (which is not necessarily a given), then he had "worshipped in fear the God who made heaven and earth" the entire time, including the point of his reenlistment as a veteran. This account seems to serve as the exception which proves the rule; unlike the other four stories of soldier-martyrs presented by Musurillo, Julius does not seem to have acted in accord with official church discipline as represented by the *Apostolic Tradition* and the other writings we've surveyed here. He had (apparently) served in battle, ostensibly including killing enemy soldiers and taking the idolatrous military oath, in contradistinction to church teaching and discipline.

However the story of Julius the veteran, rather than disproving my thesis that the church forbade converted soldiers from killing and Christians from joining the army, actually confirms it. For in this account, Julius comes to realize that his twenty-seven years of military service to Rome, presumably including fighting in Rome's wars, were in fact a "mistake" [*errare* in the Latin] in which he had served "foolishly" in the army. This is nothing short of a remarkable declaration of repentance by Julius. Here, in the last moments of his life, he had realized his grave error in apparently violating church discipline, and as an act of integrity before the commander who would soon take his life, he is announcing that he finally realizes how wrong he was to have served (and, it seems, killed) in the name of Rome.

In conclusion, it seems evident that the century of scholarship into the question of the early church and military service has largely missed the forest for the trees, so to speak. Scholars have been so caught up in gauging the number of Christians in the Roman legions in those forma-tive years that the larger issue of *why* the church objected and precisely to *what* has been ignored. The hypothesis which best explains the data is that it was not military service *as such* which the church abhorred—rather it was the *bloodshed* which is condemned in both the consensus document of the *Apostolic Tradition* and the many other citations from early church writers we have explored here.[15] Indeed, from this perspective, the num-ber of Christians serving in the army is irrelevant, for military service was tolerated in the case of converted soldiers, provided they did not kill anyone. In a widely cited conclusion that has not been significantly chal-lenged, Roland Bainton explains that

> from the end of the New Testament period to the decade AD 170–80 there is no evidence whatever of Christians in the army. The subject of military service obviously was not at that time controverted. The reason may have been either that participation was assumed or that abstention was taken for granted. The latter is more probable . . . Few as yet were converted while in the army.[16]

From that point on, the number of Christians in the army began to grow.[17] But it was not due to Christians joining the army—it was, by and large, due to the church's extraordinary evangelism efforts targeting the soldiers who oppressed them, and the remarkable testimony borne by the martyrs. The evidence from the patristic era conclusively shows that the church forbade Christians from joining the army, but tolerated converted soldiers remaining in their stations provided they did not kill anyone.

---

15. Interpreters such as John Helgeland wish to shift the grounds of the church's conscientious objection to idolatry rather than bloodshed. Without denying that the legions' idolatry was a major issue and contributed significantly to the church's stance, the many citations we have seen thus far (and those of the next part) which explicitly condemn the shedding of human blood in war, make it abundantly clear that moral and ethical scruples against killing played a vital part forming the church's conscien-tious objector stance.

16. Bainton, *Christian Attitudes toward War and Peace*, 67–68.

17. It is not important for my purposes here to document this growth; Bainton, Cadoux, Hornus, and Helgeland do this job admirably.

11

Faithful Christians Do Not Kill

*Categorical Statements on the Immorality
of Taking Human Life and the Avoidance of Blood*

THUS FAR, WE HAVE seen compelling evidence that the early church condemned the taking of human life in the specific cases of abortion/infanticide, the "spectacles" and gladiatorial combat, suicide, and killing in war. In this section, I will present and analyze some selections from the patristic literature which draw these various threads together by pointing out the moral linkage between these issues of dehumanization and violence, including a number of categorical statements that prohibit the taking of human life under any circumstances and the avoidance of blood. This "miscellaneous" section will witness to the consistent ethic of life taught and lived by the early church, and serve as a jumping-off point for the concluding sections of this research.

In the midst of a chaotic and violent third century, when the church was confronted by internal schisms from within and severe persecutions from without, Cyprian of Carthage stood as a pillar of orthodoxy and moral fortitude. In a treatise addressed to his friend Donatus, his outlook about the moral hypocrisy and bloodlust of Roman society is revealed: "The world is soaked with mutual blood," he writes, "and when individuals commit homicide, it is a crime; it is called a virtue when it is done in the name of the state. Impunity is acquired for crimes not by reason of innocence but by the magnitude of the cruelty" (*To Donatus*, 6). How consistent is it, Cyprian asks, for a society to condemn the murder of an individual by another individual, but when homicide is committed *en masse* in the name of the state, as in warfare, that same society lauds and praises the brutality which it condemns on the small scale? In Cyprian's view, this is nothing less than the sheer madness of a society which has lost its moral compass.

In his treatise on the virtue of patience, which I will examine more closely in the next section, Cyprian comments on how incredibly incompatible it is for "the hand that has held the Eucharist" to "be sullied by the blood-stained sword" (*The Good of Patience* 14). This clause does not refer to clergy alone. In those days, the consecrated elements were given directly into the communicant's hands, whereby they administered communion to themselves. This is an ordinance also concerning the laity, as the context of this treatise and sermon (addressed to everybody, including the laity) makes clear. The hands which have held the salvific blood of Christ must not be stained with the blood of another. Likewise in his personal correspondence, Cyprian expressed an uncompromising ethic of nonviolence. In a letter written at the height of one of the imperial persecutions of the 250's, he writes concerning the Christian community of Carthage that they must be ready to die as martyrs, even though church discipline prevents them from killing: "At such a time it is just not possible for everyone to be gathered in one place; they must needs be killed, even though they themselves may not kill" (*Epistle 58*). In another letter, Cyprian employs *militia Christi* imagery, as he frequently does, to refer to the spiritual combat faced by the Christians as they oppose the devil and the world's evils:

> But being driven back by both the faith and the vigour of the united army he [the devil] encountered, he has realised that the soldiers of Christ are now keeping alert watch, that they are now standing at the ready for battle, that die they can, be conquered they cannot be, and that they are unconquerable just because they are unafraid to die. They do not return the attack of their attackers since it is not lawful for the innocent to kill even the guilty, but, instead, they readily surrender their lives and their blood so that they may withdraw all the more speedily from wicked and barbarous men who enjoy such scope for their wickedness and barbarity in this world today. (*Epistle 60*)

Christians are fearless in the face of death, Cyprian says, and willingly die because they know they cannot be conquered, even if they are killed. They absorb the attacks of their persecutors, because according to their faith, "it is not lawful for the innocent to kill even the guilty." This is the unqualified statement of one who rejects physical violence in all circumstances, for if even the guilty may not be killed by Christians, who is left to kill?

Tertullian, Cyprian's spiritual mentor, in his own book on "patience" is just as categorical. Writing of Christ as the example of patience and nonviolence we are to emulate, Tertullian points to Christ's example in the garden and what we should learn from it:

> Why, even when He is betrayed, when He is led like a beast to the slaughter—for thus [it is written]: "He does not open His mouth any more than does a lamb in the power of its shearer"—He who could have had if He wished, at a single word, legions upon legions of angels from heaven to assist Him did not approve of an avenging sword on the part of even one of His disciples. It was the forbearance of the Lord that was wounded in [the person of] Malchus. And so, He actually cursed for all time the works of the sword and by healing him whom He had not Himself struck, He made satisfaction by forbearance, which is the mother of mercy. (*Patience* 3)

As he did in his comments in *On Idolatry*, 19, Tertullian uses the disarming of Peter in the garden as a moral paradigm for all Christians to emulate. Since he "did not approve of an avenging sword on the part of even one of His disciples," Jesus "actually cursed for all time the works of the sword." Additionally, in his comments on the Roman spectacles, Tertullian does not merely condemn the violence he finds there, but casts aspersions over all other violence against human beings, since God did not intend for any of his creations to be used in the slaying of human beings: "You see murder committed by iron dagger, poison, or magic incantation: but iron, poisonous herbs, demons are all equally creatures of God. Yet did not the Creator design those creatures of His for man's destruction? Certainly not. He forbids man-slaying by one summary commandment: 'Thou shalt not kill'" (*The Spectacles* 2.8). Even earlier, in his *Apology*, Tertullian had made comments strongly indicative of the church's attitude toward violence. Christians are so numerous, he tells the emperor, that they could, if they wanted to and were permitted to by their faith, rise up vigorously against those who persecute them. "For what war would we not have been fit and ready, even though unequally matched in military strength, we who are so ready to be slain, were it not that, according to our rule of life, it is granted us to be killed rather than to kill?" (*Apology* 37.4–5). Such a revolt is of course, impossible for Christians of Tertullian's day, since they may be killed, though they themselves may not kill.

Lactantius as well comments on the impossibility of Christians rising up violently against their persecutors. Despite the fact that they are being murdered wholesale by their persecutors, violent rebellion is not an option, for "Religion ought to be defended, not by killing, but by dying, not by fury, but by patience [*patientia*], not by crime but by faith. The former action each time belongs to evil, the latter to good, and it is necessary that good be the practice of religion, not evil. If you wish, indeed, to defend religion by blood, if by torments, if by evil, then, it will not be defended, but it will be violated" (*Divine Institutes* 5.19). He goes even further, later in the *Divine Institutes*. In perhaps the most categorical statement prohibiting the shedding of human blood in all circumstances from the early church, he writes,

> For when God forbids killing, He not only prohibits us from free-booting, which is not permitted even by public laws, but He also advises that those things also, which are regarded as lawful among men, should not be done. So, neither will it be permitted a just man, whose service is justice herself, to enter military service, nor can he accuse anyone of a capital crime, because there is no difference whether you kill a man with a sword or a word, since the killing itself is prohibited. Therefore, in this command of God, no exception whatsoever must be made. It is always wrong to kill a man whom God has intended to be a sacrosanct creature. (*Divine Institutes* 6.20)

Origen too had the propensity for categorical statements about never killing human beings. Celsus had said that Jesus should have revealed himself to everyone while he was on earth. Origen responded that God was preparing the world for the peaceful message of Christ by ensuring that the *Pax Romana* spread across the whole known world, minimizing the conflicts between nations that would have hindered the spread of the Christian gospel message. "Accordingly, how could this teaching, which preaches peace and does not even allow men to take vengeance on their enemies, have had any success unless the international situation had everywhere been changed and a milder spirit prevailed at the advent of Jesus?" (*Against Celsus* 2.30). Concerning the Christian teaching, "which preaches peace" and forbids violent vengeance on enemies, Origen later in that same work goes on to point out that Jesus "did not consider it compatible with his inspired legislation to allow the taking of human life in any form at all" (*Against Celsus* 3.7).

Another interesting facet about the early Christian ethic is that not only was the church adamantly opposed to Christians spilling blood, but frequent evidence throughout the patristic writings demonstrates that the early church was *so* opposed to bloodshed, that this would manifest as an aversion to blood itself. For example, Minicius Felix's character Octavius, indicates the sharp contrast between the pagans, whose lives are all but bathed in blood, and the Christians who go to great extremes to avoid blood: "But for us it is not right either to look at or to hear of acts of manslaughter; in fact, we are so careful to avoid human blood that in our meals we do not allow even the blood of edible animals" (*Octavian* 30). Lactantius likewise decries the hypocrisy of their pagan persecutors who "call impious those who are certainly pious [the Christians] and who keep away from human blood" (*Divine Institutes* 5.9). Similarly, Clement of Alexandria commented in his elucidation of Christ as an educator, "Yet it is not right for man to touch blood either, for his own body is nothing less than flesh quickened by blood. Human blood has its portion of reason, and its share in grace, along with the spirit. If anyone injures it, he will not escape punishment" (*Christ the Educator* 3.3).

Where do these strange, seemingly puritanical attitudes about blood come from? The answer lies in the early church's exegesis of the apostolic decree of Acts 15:23–29. In that circular letter, the apostles wrote to the local Gentile believers of their decision that the Gentiles should not be burdened with the entire weight of the Mosaic law, but only that they "abstain from food sacrificed to idols, from blood, from the meat of strangled animals and from sexual immorality" (Acts 15:29). The requirement to abstain from "blood" has been read in two different ways throughout the history of the church. The one which has ultimately become the dominant reading in modernity says that this is an allusion to the Torah dietary restrictions of eating meat with its blood still in it, or from eating blood (e.g., Lev 7:26–27). Yet if this is the case, why does the Acts text not indicate that this refers to "eating" blood, as the Leviticus text does? This question, coupled with the bare mention of simply avoiding "blood" gave rise to an alternate interpretation, which predominated in the early church. Tertullian's is the most explicit treatment of this interpretation: "It is sufficient that here, too, adultery and fornication have the place of honor reserved for them between idolatry and murder. For the 'prohibition of blood' we shall understand as referring much more properly to human blood" (*On Modesty* 12). The early church read the command to abstain from "blood" in Acts 15:29 to be not a kosher dietary restriction, concerned with what is proper to eat (akin to the prohibition of food sacrificed to idols and meat of strangled animals), but a *moral* restriction concerning how to treat other people (like the command to abstain from sexual immorality, also in the passage). On this reading, abstaining from "blood" in this context means abstaining from *human* blood—not killing people. This exegetical foundation (whatever we may happen to think of it) drove the early church to an avoidance of human blood altogether.

We have observed thus far that the early church was adamantly opposed to killing human beings under *any* circumstances. Christians who followed the way of Jesus just did not kill. Rather than confining the term "pro-life" into the narrow issue of abortion as we do today, the church consistently rejected killing—whether in the womb, in the arena, on the battlefield, or anywhere else. The comments of Athenagoras are appropriate to close out this section. Referring to the church's holistic, consistently pro-life ethic, he insists that Christians "are always consistent, everywhere the same, obedient to our rule and not masters of it" (*Embassy for Christians* 35).

12

The Virtue of Patience

The Positive Christian Ethic

We have so far observed a primarily negative facet of the early Christian ethic—they would not kill anyone under any circumstances. But if that is the case, how did they respond to evil and violence in their midst? The overwhelming answer attested to by their writings is a deep and abiding obedience to the nonviolence taught by the Sermon on the Mount, as well as promoting the virtue known as *hypomonē* (Greek) or *patientia* (Latin). These two words connote similar, if not identical meanings in their respective languages—longsuffering, forbearance, patient endurance, and deferring personal revenge in favor of God's vindicating justice. For convenience, the words are generally translated into English as "patience," but the virtue carried much more significance than the word "patience" would seem to suggest.[1] It meant putting up with the temporal evil perpetrated against oneself by an oppressor in the sure knowledge that God would repay the evildoer for insults and injuries done against God's holy ones. Refusal to strike back violently in kind was an essential component of this "patience," for numerous Scriptural passages[2] forbid returning violence in kind in order to avenge oneself.

Yet this was not a posture or an ethic of weakness, but rather of strength; it was disciplined and principled nonviolence, not cowardice. Patience, when combined with the hope of the kingdom, was a cardinal virtue. Its reach extended even beyond the ethical realm of responding to persecution and suffering for doing good; as we will see, it was an attitude which permeated every facet of early Christian trust in God. This

1. For this discussion of "patience," I am indebted to Hornus, *It Is Not Lawful for Me to Fight*, 214.

2. E.g., Matt 5:38–48; Rom 12:14–21; 1 Pet 2:21–25, 3:9.

included the deferment of divine rewards from this finite live to the ever-lasting life of the resurrection as well as, as Rom 12:19 says, giving up the "right" of violent self-defense so that God's divine prerogative might not be usurped.

This virtue finds its most concrete scriptural manifestation in Matt 5:38–48. These precepts included the famous turning the other cheek, going the second mile, giving more than your persecutor demands of you, and truly loving your enemies with concrete *agape* awareness of their well-being. Not surprisingly, almost every discussion of Christian behavior and response to evil included at least an allusion to this passage, if not an outright, lengthy quotation. The Sermon's ethic of nonretaliation and love of enemies was the *sine qua non* of characteristically Christian discipleship.

This is the case from the earliest days after the close of the canon. For example, in the late 1st century discipleship manual known as the *Didache* almost the entirety of chapter one is taken up by commands lifted directly from the Sermon on the Mount. For example:

> When anyone gives you a blow on the right cheek, turn to him the other as well, and be perfect; when anyone forces you to go one mile with him, go two with him; when anyone takes your cloak away, give him your coat also; when anyone robs you of your property, demand no return. You really cannot do it. Give to everyone that asks you, and demand no return; the Father wants His own bounties to be shared with all. (*Didache* 1.4–5)

For the Didachist, the "way of life" was equivalent to concrete obedience to Jesus' precepts and patient endurance of unjust suffering.

The entire apologetical strategy of Athenagoras' *Embassy for Christians* is likewise centered on concrete obedience to the Sermon on the Mount. Christians cannot be guilty of the public violence and other crimes of which they are unjustly accused, for their discipline forbids it. The Christians, he says, "have learnt not to strike back when we are flogged, nor to go to law with those who rob and despoil us. When they abuse us and strike us on one cheek, we let them strike the other, too, and if they snatch our tunic from us, we give them our cloak besides" (*Embassy for Christians* 1). Later in the apology, in reply to the frequently-leveled charge that Christians are atheists (because they did not worship the Roman pantheon or bow down to the visible statues of the gods),

Athenagoras points to the amazing, almost other-worldly nature of the Christians' ethic as proof that their convictions are given by God, and thus, they are not atheists:

> By the dogmas to which we give our assent, not man-made but divine and taught by God, we are able to persuade you that you have not to regard us as you would atheists. What are those sayings on which we are brought up? I shall tell you: "Love your enemies; bless them that curse you; pray for them that persecute you, that you may be the children of your Father who is in heaven, who maketh his sun to rise upon the good and the bad, and raineth upon the just and the unjust." (*Embassy* 11)

At this point, Athenagoras himself goes on the rhetorical attack. Which of those who are esteemed as sophisticated "philosophers" conduct themselves as virtuously as even simple Christian peasants do?

> Which of those who reduce syllogisms or explain equivocal terms or trace out etymologies or tell us of synonyms or homonyms, of categories and axioms, of subject and predicate, will undertake to render happy their associates through these and suchlike lessons, being so purified in soul as to love enemies rather than to hate them and to bless those who are forward with their revilings instead of, as would be most reasonable, answering them back, and to pray for those who plot against their lives? On the contrary, such men are ever busy wickedly paying back things spoken ill of themselves; and, being eager to work some mischief, they make their trade an artifice of words and not a manifestation of their deeds. But amongst us you might find simple folk, artisans and old women, who, if they are unable to furnish in words the assistance they derive from our doctrine, yet show in their deeds the advantage to others that accrues from their resolution. They do not rehearse words but show forth good deeds; struck, they do not strike back, plundered, they do not prosecute; to them that ask they give, and they love their neighbors as themselves. (*Embassy* 11)

He tears down the reputations of the pagan world's most respected pillars of wisdom and virtue by pointing out that the uneducated "simple folk, artisans and old women" do not revenge themselves, do not contribute to the endless cycle of violence. Finally, in the section in which he defends the Christians' consistently pro-life ethic, Athenagoras stresses the moral imperative of long-suffering and forbearance, rather than retaliation, as an essential component to the Christian way of life: "We, on the other hand, are not allowed to withdraw ourselves when struck nor may we refrain from blessing when cursed. It is not enough for us to be just (and justice is to give as good as we get); no, we must be good and long-suffering" (*Embassy* 34). The Greek word Athenagoras uses for "long-suffering" here is *hypomonē*, the same word used throughout the book of Revelation to stress patient endurance on the part of the martyrs as they await God's vindicating justice.

Also in the second century, Irenaeus stressed the need for forbearance and a rejection of violent revenge, based on the model taught in the Sermon on the Mount. In his *Proof of the Apostolic Preaching*, he contrasts the letter of the Mosaic Law with the spirit of the Christians' practices which far surpass the requirements of the Law. Christians, he says, have no need of the law as a teacher anymore, for their very character, virtue, and discipline so far exceed the law's demands that the law is obsolete in Christian fellowships:

> Therefore also we have no need of the law as pedagogue. Behold, we speak with the Father and stand face to face with Him, become infants in malice, and made strong in all justice and propriety. For no more shall the law say "Thou shalt not commit adultery" to him who has not even conceived the desire of another's wife; or "thou shalt not kill" to him who has put away from himself all anger and enmity; "thou shalt not covet thy neighbor's field, or his ox, or his ass" to those who make no account whatsoever of earthly things, but heap up profit in heaven. Nor "an eye for an eye and a tooth for a tooth" to him who counts no man his enemy, but all his neighbors, and therefore cannot even put forth his hand to revenge. (*Proof of the Apostolic Preaching* 96)

With respect to the old *lex talionis* ("eye-for-eye and tooth for tooth"), Christians no longer need it as a restriction on vengeance, Irenaeus says, because they harbor no thoughts of revenge in their hearts at all and count no one as enemies.

Justin Martyr similarly points to the absolute necessity of being long-suffering as a condition of being an authentic disciple of Jesus:

> And concerning our being long-suffering and servants to all and free from anger, this is what He said: "to him that smites you on the one cheek, offer also the other; and to him that takes away your shirt do not forbid your cloak also. And whosoever shall be angry is in the danger of the fire. And whosoever compels you to

go one mile, follow him for two. And let your good works shine before men, that they, seeing them, may wonder at your Father who is in heaven." For we ought not to quarrel; neither has He desired us to imitate wicked people, but He has exhorted us to lead all people, by patience and gentleness, from shame and evil desires. And this indeed we can show in the case of many who were once of your way of thinking, but have turned from the way of violence and tyranny, being conquered, either by the constancy of life which they have traced in [Christian] neighbors, or by the strange endurance which they have noticed in defrauded fellow travelers or have experienced in those with whom they had dealings. (*First Apology* 16)

Notice here how Justin also points to the transformative power of the teaching of the Sermon on the Mount. Those who followed "the way of violence and tyranny" have been overcome by the quality of life of their Christian neighbors, or by the "strange endurance" which they observe in those whom they counter. This "strange endurance," so unlike what is to be observed elsewhere in the Greco-Roman world, is the cardinal virtue that makes Christians who they are and when practiced consistently, overcomes the unbelief of the world.

Lactantius, whom we earlier observed forcefully propounding the Christians' absolutely pro-life ethic in all circumstances, likewise has much to say concerning the virtue of patience and the nonviolence of the Sermon on the Mount. First, in his discussion of the ethics of the world, Lactantius brings to the reader's attention the words of Cicero's *On Duties*: "If anyone should wish to unravel the complicated notion of his soul let him teach himself that he is a good man who is of help to whomever he can, and who harms no one unless he himself is harassed by injury." According to any pagan philosopher or secular ethicist, these are good and admirable sentiments—that a good person doesn't harm anyone unless that person has first been harmed by someone else. Yet for Christians, such even reasonable sentiments are intolerable. "How he corrupts a true and simple statement by the addition of two words!"[3] complains Lactantius,

For what has been the need of adding that "unless harassed by injury"? What is that he might attach vice to a good man as though it

---

3. Cicero's clause "'unless harassed by injury" is composed of only two words in the Latin.

were a most disgraceful tail, and to cause him to have no part with patience, which is the greatest of all virtues? He said that a good man would harm if he had been harassed. Now from this very act, if he should do harm, he would of necessity lose the name of a good man. For it is no less an evil to pay back an injury than to inflict one . . . (*Divine Institutes* 6.18)

In Lactantius' judgment, Cicero has utterly ruined his otherwise admirable ethic by admitting the possibility of violent revenge and returning harm in kind. Calling patience [*patientia*] "the greatest of all virtues," Lactantius says that Cicero has sacrificed all connection to the Christian virtue when he allows for harming others in return for harm received, for paying back an injury in kind is, in Christian estimation, just as evil as causing the initial harm in the first place. This is because "he who strives to repay an injury throws himself out of the way to imitate the very one by whom he has been wounded. Thus, he who imitates evil can in no way be good. Therefore, by those two words he took away from a good and wise man the two greatest virtues: innocence and patience" (*Divine Institutes* 6.18). For Lactantius, the virtue of patience is an act of mastery over the self and over one's own violent impulses: "But if, when harassed by injury, he begin to pursue the one who is hurting him [in violence], he has been conquered; but he who represses that movement by reason, clearly he is master of himself, he is able to rule himself. This withholding of oneself is rightly called patience which is one virtue opposed to all vices and passions" (ibid.).

Two Christian writers of the third century wrote entire treatises elucidating the virtue of *patientia*: Tertullian and Cyprian. Cyprian's treatise is closely patterned after Tertullian's, so I will focus more closely on the latter's treatise, but Cyprian's thoughts are also worth briefly exploring first. Recognizing the necessity of concrete obedience to the precepts of the Sermon on the Mount, Cyprian points to patience as that which makes obedience to Jesus possible in the first place:

How then will you be able to endure these things—not to swear or curse, not to seek again what has been taken away from you, on receiving a blow to offer the other cheek also to your assailant, to forgive your brother who offends you not only seventy times seven times, but all his offenses without exception, to love your enemies, to pray for your adversaries and persecutors, if you do not have the steadfastness of patience and forbearance? (*The Good of Patience* 16)

Patience seems to be a broad umbrella virtue, under which the praxis of nonviolence would be included as a practical subset. In another treatise, this one addressed to Demetrian, the African proconsul responsible for violent local persecutions of the Carthaginian Christians, Cyprian tells of the reason Christians are able to be long-suffering, patient, and nonviolent, even in the midst of savage persecution: "Cease to injure the servants of God and of Christ with your persecutions for when they are injured divine vengeance defends them. For this reason it is that no one of us fights back when he is apprehended, nor do our people avenge themselves against your unjust violence though numerous and plentiful. Our certainty of the vengeance which is to come makes us patient" (*To Demetrian* 16–17). God's promise that he will avenge the unjust suffering of his saints (Cf. Rev 6:9–11) is what gives the Christians hope and enables them to live lives of patient endurance in the face of unjust suffering.

Tertullian's treatise on *patientia* likewise demonstrates how his keen legally-educated mind was deeply formed by the nonviolence and patience taught by the Sermon on the Mount. Elucidating on patience in the teaching of Jesus, Tertullian teaches,

> If one tries to provoke you to a fight, there is at hand the admonition of the Lord: "If someone strike thee," He says, "on the right cheek, turn to him the other also." Let wrong-doing grow weary from your patience: whoever be struck, the one who strikes, weighed down by pain and shame, will suffer more severely from the Lord: by your meekness you will strike a more severe blow to the wrong-doer; for he will suffer at the hands of Him by whose grace you practice meekness." (*Patience* 8.2)

The strength of the one practicing the virtue of patience is said to overpower and wear down the assaults of the aggressor. Notice also the threat of divine vengeance which he, like Cyprian, holds over the heads of the unjust oppressors as the cause of the strength of the practice of patient nonviolence.

Impatience on the other hand, Tertullian goes on to say, such as when Peter attempted to violently defend his master in the garden of Gethsemane, is the root of all sin. "Impatience is, as it were, the original sin in the eyes of the Lord," he explains. "For, to put it in a nutshell, every sin is to be traced back to impatience" (*Patience* 5.21). And violence, which Christians condemn and reject as acceptable for disciples of Christ, is the fruit of impatience: "Now, nothing undertaken through impatience can be transacted without violence, and everything done with violence has either met with no success or has collapsed or has plunged to its own destruction." (*Patience* 10.8). But God has so demonstrated his forbearance and long-suffering throughout salvation history so as to leave a model for God's people to emulate. Despite the frequent relapses of his chosen people into idolatry and disloyalty, God delays his judgment on them for centuries in the hopes that they will return to be his faithful covenant people once more. In doing so, Tertullian explains, it has been revealed that "Patience is the very nature of God" (*Patience* 3).

Patience, *patientia*, or *hypomonē* thus stands firmly at the center of the early church's ethic. Their other-worldly forbearance and long-suffering in the face of evil earned them deep suspicion on the part of their pagan neighbors, but also even deeper respect and admiration, opening up avenues for curious inquirers to be taught about the God whose very nature is patience, slow to anger but abounding in steadfast love, and about the Savior who epitomized patience and nonviolence in his endurance of the cross for the salvation of the world.

13

Realized Eschatology

The Early Church as the Fulfillment of Isaiah 2:1–5[1]

HAVING TRACED THE EARLY church's consistently pro-life ethic including a refusal to kill under any circumstances and positive response to evil in the form of obedience to the Sermon on the Mount and the virtue of patience, it's time to look briefly at the importance of this stance for the cause of biblical interpretation and lived theology in the Christian community. In this section, we will explore the development of an important theme as the leaders of the early Christian church make explicit what to now has been only implicit: that wherever God's reign is manifested in the church, there Christ's normative peace also resides. Specifically, we will trace how the amazing oracle found in Isa 2:1–5 with its prediction of the end of violence and warfare, was understood as having come to its fulfillment in the midst of Christ's followers.[2] This in turn, will offer us crucial guidance as we evaluate how Christian disciples are to live with respect to the question of violence.

The early church leaders were well-acquainted with the Hebrew Scriptures, but believed that they held a different message for their own time. Sitting as they did on the other side of the resurrection of Christ, they saw in Jesus the key to comprehending the haunting oracle of Isaiah. The first Christian author to explicitly cite Isa 2:1–5 is Justin Martyr, in approximately 150. In chapter 39 of his *First Apology*, he attempts to show

---

1. This chapter is adapted from Part III of my *Proclaiming the Gospel of Peace.*

2. It is worth noting here that Isaiah's vision of beating swords into plowshares and heralding the end of violence and warfare is one of the most frequently quoted Old Testament passages the early church leaders drew upon to demonstrate the nature of the church's nonviolent, realized eschatology.

the validity of the Christian faith by appealing to the action of the Holy Spirit through prophecy fulfillment. He explains:

> When the prophetic Spirit speaks as prophesying things to come, he says: "For the law will go forth from Zion and the Word of the Lord from Jerusalem, and he shall judge in the midst of the nations and rebuke much people; and they shall beat their swords into plowshares and their spears into pruning hooks, and nation will not lift up sword against nation, neither shall they learn to war anymore." We can show you that this has really happened . . . and [now] we who once killed each other not only do not make war on each other, but in order not to lie or deceive our inquisitors we gladly die for the confession of Christ. (*First Apology* 39)

After citing Isaiah's prophecy, Justin here explicitly connects its fulfillment with the peaceable actions and teachings of Christ's apostles, who not only no longer murder and wage war on their enemies, but willingly suffer martyrdom as a witness to their faith. Justin also repeats this affirmation in a similar context in his *Dialogue with Trypho*. After citing Mic 4:1–7 (the verbal parallel to Isa 2:1–5) in the previous chapter, he says that that prophecy has been fulfilled in the nonviolent Christians:

> For we, who have come to know the true worship of God from the Law, and the Word that went forth from Jerusalem by the apostles of Jesus, have fled for refuge to Him who is God of Jacob and God of Israel. And we who were filled full of war, and slaughter one of another, and every kind of evil, have from out of the whole earth each changed our weapons of war, our swords into ploughshares and our pikes into farming tools, and we farm piety, righteousness, the love of man, faith, and hope which comes from the Father Himself through Him who was crucified, each of us dwelling under his own vine, that is, each enjoying only his own wedded wife. (*Dialogue with Trypho* 110.2–3)

His statements here affirms two essential beliefs common to the leaders of the early church, namely that murder and warfare are expressly forbidden for the followers of Christ, and second, that the shalom-filled lives of the Christians of Justin's day are evidence that the word spoken by Isaiah had indeed come to pass through the work of the servant-king Jesus.

Irenaeus, bishop of Lyons, shares Justin's sentiments. One of the targets of his *Against Heresies*, the followers of Marcion, charged that the

God revealed in the Hebrew Scriptures was a lesser and inferior god than Jesus' *Abba* in the New Testament. To refute this claim, Irenaeus pointed to the use of the Hebrew prophetic literature by the Christian writers of the New Testament, and to the ultimate fulfillment of all the messianic prophecies by Jesus. Of particular note to this study is his use of the Isaiah 2 prophecy:

> [B]ut from the Lord's advent, the new covenant which brings back peace, and the law which gives life, has gone forth over the whole earth, as the prophets said: "For out of Zion shall go forth the law, and the word of the Lord from Jerusalem; and He shall rebuke many people; and they shall break down their swords into ploughshares, and their spears into pruning-hooks, and they shall no longer learn to fight." (*Against Heresies* 4.34.4)

Of note in this quotation is first, the affirmation that the Lord *is* the inauguration of the new covenant, and second, that his law has *already* "gone forth over the whole earth," and that this law is to be identified with the word of the Lord in Isaiah 2. He continues:

> If therefore another law and word, going forth from Jerusalem, brought in such a [reign of] peace among the Gentiles which received it (the word), and convinced, through them, many a nation of its folly, then [only] it appears that the prophets spoke of some other person. But if the law of liberty, that is, the word of God, preached by the apostles (who went forth from Jerusalem) throughout all the earth, caused such a change in the state of things, that these [nations] did form the swords and war-lances into ploughshares, and changed them into pruning-hooks for reaping the corn, [that is], into instruments used for peaceful purposes, and that they are now unaccustomed to fighting, but when smitten, offer also the other cheek, then the prophets have not spoken these things of any other person, but of Him who effected them. This person is our Lord ... (*Against Heresies* 4.34.4)

In this section, Irenaeus creates a hypothetical situation in which the accusations of the Marcionites can be substantiated. The evidence to support or deny their view would be in the results lived by the recipients of the prophecy. If they live peaceful, loving lives, then the accusations of the Marcionites are refuted. As proof of this outcome, Irenaeus lifts up, as Justin before him had done, the practical results of the Christian convictions on the lives of believers. Two notable conclusions can be drawn from this affirmation. First: he describes the *de facto* behavior of the Christians of his day. They have turned their war instruments into tools of cultivation, are "unaccustomed to fighting," and literally offer the other cheek when they are struck. Second: Irenaeus tells us that the peaceable lives of Christian believers demonstrate that the prophet was indeed typologically speaking of Jesus Christ. The renunciation of violence by faithful followers of Jesus thus serves a crucial apologetic purpose in establishing the truthfulness of Christian claims. If the church of Jesus Christ is living without war and violence, then the prophecy is fulfilled. Without this embodied peace in the Christian community, such apologetic claims are destroyed and Christian claims about Jesus' messiahship lose their credibility.

Tertullian was likewise familiar with the passage, and used it frequently throughout his work to illustrate the effects of the "law of Christ." He sought to demonstrate that with regard to the Mosaic Law, the ethic of Christ was an entirely new law. After quoting the Isaiah passage in a treatise against Jewish objections to Christianity, he notes:

> Who else, therefore, are understood but we, who, fully taught by the new law, observe these practices,—the old law being obliterated, the coming of whose abolition the action itself demonstrates? For the wont of the old law was to avenge itself by the vengeance of the glaive, and to pluck out "eye for eye," and to inflict retaliatory revenge for injury. But the new law's wont was to point to clemency, and to convert to tranquility the pristine ferocity of "glaives" and "lances," and to remodel the pristine execution of "war" upon the rivals and foes of the law into the pacific actions of "ploughing" and "tilling" the land. (Tertullian, *An Answer to the Jews*, 3)

Whatever we may think of his attitude regarding the Hebraic Law, it is clear from this passage that he believes that with Christ, a new era has begun, which is marked not by retaliatory vengeance and retributive justice, but by "tranquility" and "clemency."

Tertullian also wrote against Marcion and employed much the same strategy as that done by Irenaeus before him. He cited messianic prophecies in the Hebrew Scriptures, and pointed out their fulfillment in the peaceful and enemy-loving lives of the Christians, whom he regarded as the true inheritors of the prophetic fulfillment. One exemplary passage, utilizes Isaiah 2 to just this effect:

> The gospel will be this "way," of the new law and the new word in Christ, no longer in Moses. "And He shall judge among the na-

tions," even concerning their error. "And these shall rebuke a large nation," that of the Jews themselves and their proselytes. "And they shall beat their swords into ploughshares, and their spears into pruning-hooks"; in other words, they shall change into pursuits of moderation and peace the dispositions of injurious minds, and hostile tongues, and all kinds of evil, and blasphemy. "Nation shall not lift up sword against nation," shall not stir up discord. "Neither shall they learn war any more," that is, the provocation of hostilities; so that you here learn that Christ is promised not as powerful in war, but pursuing peace . . .

Verily the apostles have annulled that belief of yours. (*Against Marcion*, 3.21)

Countering Marcion's assertion that the Hebrew prophets had been inspired by some lesser god, Tertullian takes this ancient prophecy of hope in Yahweh and applies it to what has already been accomplished through Jesus Christ. In explicating this passage from Isaiah, he hopes to show the remarkable continuity between the Old Covenant and the New, and to refute those who posited an inferior god. In Tertullian's view, this continuity is evident in the lives of the Christians of his era, who do not "lift up sword" or "learn war" anymore. Similarly, Tertullian goes on to note the fulfillment of another Isaiahic oracle, Isa 52:7—"You can see also how there were prophecies of the work of the apostles: 'How beautiful are the feet of them that preach the gospel of peace, that preach the gospel of good things,' not of war or of evil things" (*Against Marcion* 3.22). Christ's apostles are those spoken of by Isaiah who "preach the gospel of peace," and not of war or other evils.

These are but some of the examples of the citations of this particular prophecy by leaders of the early church.[3] What then can be concluded from this survey? Extant documents from the leaders of the early church are unanimous in their belief that this prophecy had *already been fulfilled* through the incarnation of Christ and the followers who patterned their loving, peaceful existence by his life and teachings.[4] The forcefulness with

3. Origen is another example of an early church father who believed this prophecy had been fulfilled through the coming of Christ. See *Against Celsus* 5.33 for one further example.

4. The consistently nonviolent, pacifist interpretation of the Isaiah 2 prophecy waned and ultimately disappeared however, with the establishment of Christianity as the Empire's official religion. Eusebius of Caesarea, Athanasius, and other post-Constantinian church fathers interpreted Isaiah 2:1–5 in light of the Constantinian "peace," which they believed was the culmination of the peaceable ends to which the gospel was leading. For example,

which they argued for the prophetic fulfillment of "all things" through Jesus Christ is quite evident in these brief selections from their work. It was their firm conviction that Jesus has come, and the "last days" spoken of by Isaiah are indeed upon us.

In his discussion of the patristic exegesis of Isaiah 2, Gerhard Lohfink astutely points out some of the reasons the early leaders of the church were willing to make this bold claim of prophetic fulfillment. First he notes, it was not only the view of the early church fathers and mothers that the time of the ingathering of the nations foretold in Isa 2:2–3 had arrived in the inclusion of Gentiles in the reconstituted people of God, but also that *"the eschatological state of nonviolence and peace, prophesied by Isaiah, had already become reality in the church."*[5] The church leaders were able to point to the fact that the Christians renounced all forms of violence as evidence that the prophecy had been fulfilled, at least in part. Second, the fact of this fulfillment was tremendously important for the early apologists in their discourses with non-messianic Jews, such as Justin's *Dialogue with Trypho*, the Jew. Lohfink's summary of the import of this fulfillment in apologetic discourse is worth citing at length:

> The "fulfillment exegesis" of Isaiah 2 is originally set in dispute with Judaism; this is evident in Justin, Irenaeus, and Tertullian. The Jews argue quite correctly that if nothing in the world has been changed, the Messiah cannot have come. If the Messiah had come, then at least the prophecy of peace in Isaiah 2:4 would have become reality. Yet, they say, there is no indication that this has occurred. The world is still full of war; men still fight their battles. So Jesus of Nazareth cannot have been the Messiah . . . The reply of the early church Fathers to the central Jewish objection to Christianity . . . is rather that the Messiah has come and that the world has in fact changed. It has been transformed *in the Messiah's people*, which lives in accord with the law of Christ. There is no longer any violence in the messianic people, the church. There, all

Eusebius was so won over by the grandeur of the "Christian" Empire that it permeated his writings. This citation from his *Preparation for the Gospel* should suffice to illustrate this subtle, but critical shift:

> That which the prophecies have foretold has been fulfilled precisely. The various independent governments were destroyed by the Romans; and Augustus became the sole master of the entire universe the moment when our Savior came down to earth. Since that time, no nation has waged war on another nation, and life is no longer squandered in the former confusion.

5. Lohfink, *Jesus and Community*, 173 (emphasis original).

have become "sons of peace" (Luke 10:6). There, people prefer to be struck on the other cheek rather than to retaliate (Matt. 5:39). There, the making of war has been unlearned. Isaiah 2 has already been fulfilled in the church.[6]

This claim, in other words, is central to the perceptions those outside the church form about the veracity of Christian truth claims. Justin, Irenaeus, Tertullian, and the rest were able to point to the nonviolence of the church of their era as evidence that the church exists as the firstfruits of the fulfillment of this oracle. So confident were they in the lives of the saints as evidence of the messianic fulfillment on these grounds, that Origen was able to claim, "No longer do we take the sword against any nation, nor do we learn war any more, since we have become sons of peace through Jesus."[7]

This answer to the Jewish objection is, of course, quite perilous. It assumes the *continued* fidelity of the Christian church to the way of Jesus exemplified in Christ's passion and vindicated in the resurrection. Indeed, the whole of Christology is undermined if outsiders are unable to look at the life of the church and see in its nonviolence the fulfillment of Isaiah's oracle, for if we are unable to point to a peaceable Christian church to substantiate our claims, how can we credibly say that Messiah *has* come, if wars and violence continue even in our own midst? Our claims about Jesus ring hollow and empty to skeptical ears if we do not embody the peace and nonviolence which Isaiah foretold that the Messiah would bring.

6. Ibid., 175.

7. Origen, *Against Celsus*, 5.33 (cited in Lohfink, *Jesus and Community*, 175).

14

Martyrdom and the Way of the Cross

B EFORE CLOSING THIS INQUIRY into ancient Christian ethics, one subject remains to be explored—the Christian attitude toward martyrdom. I have already touched upon some issues relating to Christian martyrdom, such as the idea of martyrdom as spiritual "combat" and the Christians' willingness (and in some cases, eagerness) to die witnessing for their faith. In this section, I will go deeper into these themes, exploring their impact on the church's attitude toward death.

It must be remembered however that death, even death for the faith, was not the most important part of martyrdom. The word "martyr" comes from the Greek for "witness," or "testimony," and this was the essential part of martyrdom. As one commentator puts it, "Death did *not* make one a martyr. Witnessing, testifying, publicly arguing for and defending the validity of ideas made one a martyr."[1] The gospel of John for example uses Greek verb *martureō* (bear witness, testify) over twenty times, but not in reference to death. However by the late first century, being a *martys* (witness) had started to become a technical term in Christian circles, often referring to those who "bore witness" to the truth of their faith by the manner of their death. For example, using the verb *martureō*, Clement of Rome writes of the witness-bearing deaths of Peter and Paul as paradigmatic for Christians to emulate in their discipleship walk:

> Let us set before our eyes the noble apostles: Peter, who by reason
> of wicked jealousy, not only once or twice but frequently endured
> suffering and thus, *bearing his witness*, went to the glorious place
> which he merited. By reason of rivalry and contention Paul showed
> how to win the prize for patient endurance.[2] Seven times he was

1. Ronsse, "Rhetoric of Martyrs," 284.

2. The Greek here is *hypomonē*, the same word I stressed in the last section. Patient endurance and martyrdom were thus closely bound up together in the ethic of the early church.

> in chains; he was exiled, stoned, became a herald [of the gospel] in East and West, and won the noble renown which his faith merited. To the whole world he taught righteousness, and reaching the limits of the West *he bore his witness* before rulers. And so, released from this world, he was taken up into the holy place and became the greatest example of patient endurance. (*1 Clement* 5)

Bearing witness to the truth of the faith was regarded as one of the highest virtues in the early church, and believers sought out every conceivable opportunity to do so. In the first few centuries of the church's persecuted, precarious existence, this opportunity was often granted by the hostile persecutions the church was to endure.

Imitating Paul's attitude in Phil 1:21–24, the early Christians despised death, knowing it had been defeated and robbed of its sting by the Savior. Through their practice of the virtue of patience, their eyes were set on the life to come as immeasurably greater and richer than even the best of this world. Athenagoras explained that Christians "consider life in this world as brief and of little worth" compared to the life to come (*Embassy for Christians*, 12). Cyprian likewise, writing to encourage his fellow imprisoned confessors and to strengthen them for the deadly ordeal that awaited them, wrote of the promise which awaited the martyrs on the other side of their fiery trial:

> You happily live in daily expectation of the blessed day of your departure, ready at any moment to quit this world and impatient to reach your dwelling place with God and the rewards of your martyrdom. After the darkness of this universe, you are about to behold the most brilliant of light and to receive a glory that outshines all struggles and sufferings. (*Epistle 76*)

This despising of the world for the sake of the life to come both edified the martyrs and emboldened them to speak of their certainty that they would receive the promise of eternal life from the Lord. This excerpt from the account of the death of Justin Martyr shows the saint's unwavering surety and faith in God for redemption:

> Having for a long time become aware of the attitude of the saints, the magistrate once again met to speak with then, and addressed Justin: "You who are called eloquent, and who believe you understand the true doctrines, listen: if you are scourged and beheaded, do you suppose that you will really ascend into heaven, as you

think, and that you will receive the reward of good things, as you teach?"

"I do not merely suppose it," said the saint, "but I know it certainly and am fully assured of it." (*The Martyrdom of Justin and His Companions*, cited in Musurillo)

The earliest (and by my reckoning, the most moving) first-person account of a martyrdom comes from Ignatius, bishop of Antioch in the early part of the second century. Ignatius had been arrested and was being transported to a certain death in the "games" of the Coliseum at Rome, where he was to be torn apart by wild beasts for the amusement of the crowds. While being transported to his death, Ignatius writes in the passionate, candid and perhaps, impetuous terms of one who knows he is going to die, but who welcomes his impending death as a chance to witness to his faith. Ignatius' letters show an acute self-awareness of himself as a public figure, and he wrote to exhort his readers to be willing to imitate the passion of Jesus: "The unbelievers bear the stamp of this world, while the believers, animated by love, bear the stamp of God the Father through Jesus Christ, whose life is not in us unless we are ready of our own accord to die in order to share His Passion" (*Magnesians*, 5.2). Even as an upstanding Christian leader (and according to tradition, himself a disciple of the apostle John), Ignatius felt himself coming to a new awareness of what it means to follow Jesus as he was on the road to martyrdom. Even after a lifetime of faithfulness, only now, he says, that he is staring a martyr's death in the face, is he finally being initiated into true Christian discipleship (*Ephesians*, 3.1). Writing to the Christians in Rome he urged them not to intervene on his behalf in an attempt to save his life. He actually *wanted* to die; this was true discipleship: "Grant me no more than that you let my blood be spilled in sacrifice to God, while yet there is an altar ready" (*Romans*, 2.2). His letter betrays an eagerness to become food for the wild beasts, both so that he can witness for his faith, and so that he can be united with Jesus Christ face-to-face sooner:

> I am writing to all the Churches and state emphatically to all that I die willingly for God, provided you do not interfere. I beg you, do not show me unseasonable kindness. Suffer me to be the food of wild beasts, which are the means of making my way to God. God's wheat I am, and by the teeth of wild beasts I am to be ground that I may prove Christ's pure bread. Better still, coax the wild beasts

to become my tomb and to leave no part of my person behind. (*Romans*, 4)

And finally, in an entreaty that indicates the real reasoning behind his eagerness to suffer, Ignatius urges the Romans to "permit me to be an imitator of my suffering God!" (*Romans* 6.3). For Ignatius, the ultimate form of the imitation of Christ is to suffer as Christ suffered (1 Pet 2:21).

Like Ignatius, this robust confidence in God's vindication and promises of resurrection led other Christian martyrs to despise death and mock the cruel suffering inflicted on them by their torturers. The author of the account of Polycarp's heroic martyrdom[3] makes some important comments about the comportment and disposition of the Christian martyrs in the preface to his account:

> Blessed indeed and noble are all the martyrdoms that took place in accordance with God's will. For we must devoutly assign to God a providence over them all. Who indeed would not admire the martyrs' nobility, their courage, their love of the Master? For even when they were torn by whips until the very structure of their bodies was laid bare down to the inner veins and arteries, they endured it, making even the bystanders to weep for pity. Some indeed attained to such courage that they would utter not a sound or a cry, showing to all of us that in the hour of their torment these noblest of Christ's witnesses were not present in the flesh, or rather that the Lord was there present holding converse with them. Fixing their eyes on the favour of Christ, they despised the tortures of this world, in one hour buying themselves an exemption from the eternal fire. (*The Martyrdom of Polycarp* 2)

Cyprian too pointed out the martyrs' heroism in the face of death, while implicitly linking the suffering of the martyrs as imitation of the salvific suffering of Christ: "For the body of a Christian feels no terror at the sight of clubs, given that all his hopes in fact depend upon wood [i.e., the cross]. Indeed, the servant of Christ discerns in them a holy sign of his salvation: by wood he has been redeemed for life eternal, and by wood he has now been set on his way to win his crown" (*Epistle 76*). Finally, in the extant account of a dialogue with other Christian leaders, Origen declared his readiness and eagerness, rivaling that of Ignatius, that he too was ready to shed his own blood for Christ's sake:

3. Which is in fact, the earliest extant account of a Christian martyrdom outside of the New Testament.

And so, I am ready to die for the sake of truth; and so, in the face of so-called certain death, I scorn it; and so: Come wild beasts! Come crosses! Come fire! Come tortures! I know that as soon as it is over, I depart from my body, I am in peace with Christ. Therefore let us take up the battle, therefore let us take up the struggle, groaning at being in the body, not as if, once in the tomb, we will be back in the body, but (persuaded that) we will be set free and will exchange our body for something more spiritual. Destined as we are to be 'dissolved with Christ' (Phil 1:23), how we groan (cf. 2 Cor 5:24), we who are in the body! (*Dialogue of Origen with Hereclides* 24)

This extraordinary courage was due largely to an uncompromising refusal to fear death. To be willing to die was to be willing to go be with Christ, the very object of their fervent desire: "What place is there here for anxiety and worry? Who in the midst of these things is fearful and sad save he who lacks hope and faith? For it is for him to fear death who is unwilling to go to Christ. It is for him to be unwilling to go to Christ who does not believe that he is beginning to reign with Christ." (Cyprian *Mortality* 2). In his letters, Cyprian is no less fervent in his insistence that death is nothing to be feared for those who are in Christ:

Now, were it possible for us to escape from death, then dying would sensibly be something we might fear. But as man, being mortal, has no option but to die, then let us grasp the opportunity that now comes thanks to God's promise and providence; let us bring our lives to an end, winning at the same time the reward of immortality; let us have no fear of being put to death, since we know it is when we are put to death that we win our crowns. (*Epistle 58*)

And this amazing courage and inner strength was not confined to Christian men alone, for as Octavian tells his pagan opponent Caecilian, "Why, [even] our children and weak women are inspired with such powers of enduring suffering that they scoff at crosses and tortures, at wild beasts and all your terrifying array of torments" (Minicius Felix, *Octavius* 37).

Martyrdom, as we saw earlier, was spiritual "combat" for the early church; this, rather than with swords and bloodshed, was how Christians fought and contended for what is right and good. In his letters, Cyprian wrote passionately about how the martyrs lead the fight as soldiers for Christ and overcome the forces of the devil: "In leading the vanguard to victory over tortures they have given the others a model in fortitude and faith; they fought at the battlefront until the very battle line collapsed, vanquished" (*Epistle 10*). His depiction of the suffering of the martyrs turns graphic and grotesque, but for Cyprian, all this was to the glory of God and achieved crowns of glory and honor for the martyrs:

> Though all exposed to the weapons of this world, these believers were clad in the armour of faith. The tortured stood their ground more resolutely than their torturers; and their limbs, battered and butchered as they were, vanquished the instruments of torment as they battered and butchered them. Impregnable faith could not be stormed by the lengthy repetition of savage blows, even though, with the framework of their vitals torn apart, the servants of God no longer had limbs to offer their torturers but wounds only. There flowed blood such as to quench the blaze of persecution, to quiet with its glorious flood the flames and fires of hell. (*Epistle 10*)

Likewise in Origen's passionate and beautiful *Exhortation to Martyrdom*, he employs *militia Christi* imagery to speak of how the martyrs, far from being defeated when they are killed, actually *overcome* evil and persecutions by their deaths.

> What time could be more acceptable than when, because of our piety towards God in Christ, we make our solemn entry in this world surrounded by a guard and when we are led out, more like triumphant conquerors than conquered? For martyrs in Christ despoil with Him the principalities and powers and triumph with Him, by partaking in His sufferings and the great deeds accomplished in His sufferings—among which is His triumphing over principalities and powers, which you will soon see conquered and overcome with shame. What other day could be for us such a day of salvation as the day of so glorious a departure from here below? (*Exhortation to Martyrdom* 42)

Before ending my excursion into the psychology and theology of Christian martyrdom, one final consideration, this one apologetic in nature, seems appropriate. In his exploration into the astounding expansion of the early church,[4] sociologist Rodney Stark points to the evangelistic nature of Christian martyrdoms as one of the key facets of the church's explosive growth, without which the early Jesus movement never would have taken root in Roman society. Christian martyrs frequently died very public deaths, such as Ignatius in the Coliseum, giving them broad audi-

---

4. Stark, *Rise of Christianity*.

ences to whom they proclaimed the truth of the gospel, both in words and in the manner of their deaths. Bystanders were swayed, and the church grew by leaps and bounds thanks to the evangelistic efforts of these martyrs who were faithful unto death. The church taught that just as the blood of Christ was salvific and shed for the forgiveness of sins, the blood of those who lost their lives in public witness in imitation of Christ's passion was also redemptive: "For by this means [martyrdom], all sins are forgiven. That is why we thank you immensely for your sentences of condemnation. Such is the difference between things divine and human. When we are condemned by you, we are acquitted by God" (Tertullian *Apology* 50.16).

Tertullian also famously declared to the imperial authorities that Christians "become more numerous every time we are hewn down by you: the blood of Christians is seed" (*Apology* 50.13). This sentiment must have been widely held in the early church, for it is echoed directly in the martyrology of Apollonius:

> "Apollonius," said the proconsul Perennis, "the senate has decreed that there be no Christians."
>
> Apollonius (also called Sakkeas) said: "A divine decree cannot be quelled by a decree of man. Indeed, the more they kill those who believed in him, so much the more will their numbers grow by God's aid." (*The Martyrdom of Apollonius*, cited in Musurillo)

The church lived out the command of Christ to take up the cross and follow him down the costly road of discipleship, which frequently lead to Golgotha, and in living out their faith with integrity, and embracing what came to be seen as the "baptism of blood,"[5] the church won many converts to Christ and showed the unbelieving world the transformative power of the gospel.

---

5. On this, see for example Tertullian *Homily on Baptism* 16–17.

Conclusion

I N THIS STUDY, I have traced the ethic of the pre-Constantinian church through a series of individual moral issues related to the taking of human life, and have found that, without exception, the church strongly condemned the taking of human life in any form whatsoever. Neither homicide, nor feticide, nor infanticide, nor suicide, nor capital punishment, nor killing in war were considered acceptable to a church fiercely committed to following the teaching and moral example of the incarnate Lord.

> The same writers who opposed bloodshed in any other form also condemned abortion . . . For these people the love which obliterated distinctions between adult and child, guilty and innocent, friend and enemy also demolished the distinction between born and unborn. Christ's life and teachings raised the fetus to the status of neighbor. Abortion manifested violence and injustice to that neighbor and thus became an example of bloodshed, or murder. Those who refused to kill in war refused to kill in the womb, and vice versa.[1]

While recognizing that the differences existing between the ethic of the Old Covenant and that of the New were the result of different phases of legislation by the divine Lawgiver, the church found itself committed to a *consistently pro-life* ethic that forbade the followers of Jesus from ever killing another human being. Their response to evil was consistently *nonviolent* resistance through the virtue of patience and abiding trust in the Lord's vindicating justice.

But at the same time, as obedient servants of the One who had shed his blood for them, the early Christians were more than willing to shed their own blood in his service as a witness to their ultimate loyalty. By laying down their own lives in the service of the church as Christ had laid down his life for them, Christians imitated Christ's passion and trusted

---

1. Gorman, *Abortion & the Early Church*, 89.

in his redemption. Their startling conviction to *never* kill another human being, coupled with their readiness to bleed and die in witness to the kingdom of God marked the church off as radically different from their pagan neighbors, and witnessed to the transformed reality that is possible through Jesus Christ.

In presenting these early Christian witnesses, I do not mean to suggest that the ancient Christian church was some sort of unfallen "golden age." The ancient Christians had their own sins and failures just as we do, and that history *must* be appropriated critically if it is to be of any real value for the present. For example, while I have high regard for the ethics of violence demonstrably taught and lived by the early church, I must be on guard against a wistful romanticism which idealizes the tremendously turbulent times in which they lived. Likewise, the ancient Christians' very strict, often ascetic sexual ethic, while deeply countercultural when compared to Greco-Roman sexual and social mores, was based upon some scientific and cultural assumptions which range from the deeply questionable to the simply untrue, and which make an uncritical reappropriation of the ancient Christian sexual ethic a morally questionable enterprise. But with regard to the ancient Christian ethic of bloodshed which I have sought to demonstrate was consistently against Christians deliberately killing another human being, we ought to both measure that ethic against the teaching of the Scriptures to determine if it is indeed a faithful lived expression of Christian discipleship, as well as engage in a critical discernment of our own context to determine if embracing a consistently pro-life ethic as the ancient Christians did will lead to greater healing and peace amidst our blood-soaked world. I deeply believe that it will.

Today, those who call themselves disciples of Jesus would do well to sit as learners at the feet of the early saints, martyrs, theologians, bishops, and apologists, observe their moral clarity with regard to violence, and mimic them in their desire for obedience to Jesus. Our forbearers in the faith discerned that in their day, following Jesus meant obedience to and imitation of the paradigm of his Passion as the most redemptive and ultimately most "effective" way to combat evil. Are our times really so different as to necessitate a different course of action? We should follow the example of the early church and forswear any bloodshed but our own, and glory in none but the blood of Jesus. The closing words here belong to Arnobius of Sicca, whose *Case Against the Pagans* contrasted the great virtue of Christian praxis with the moral bankruptcy of their pagan neighbors. Christians, he says, "have learned from His teachings and His laws that evil should not be repaid with evil; that it is better to suffer wrong than be its cause, [and] to pour forth one's own blood rather than to stain our hands and conscience with the blood of another" (*The Case Against the Pagans*, 1.6).

Appendix A

Reading List of Primary Source Documents

1. 1 Clement

2. 2 Clement

3. Ignatius—Ephesians, Magnesians, Trallians, Romans, Philadelphians, Smyrnaeans, to Polycarp

4. Polycarp—To the Philippians,

5. Epistle of Barnabas

6. Didache

7. Shepherd of Hermas

8. Aristedes—Apology

9. Justin Martyr—First Apology, Second Apology, Dialogue with Trypho, Discourse Against the Greeks

10. Tatian—Address to the Greeks

11. Athenagoras—Embassy for Christians, On the Resurrection of the Dead

12. Theophilus of Antioch—Apology to Autolycus

13. Letter to Diognetus

14. Minicius Felix—Octavian

15. Irenaeus—Against Heresies, Demonstration of the Apostolic Preaching

16. Clement of Alexandria—Stromata, Exhortation to the Greeks (Heathen), Teacher (Paedogogus), Who Is the Rich Man That Is Being Saved?

17. Origen—Against Celsus, On First Principles, On Prayer, Exhortation to Martyrdom

18. Julius Africanus

19. Adamantius—De Recta in Deum Fide (Dialogue on the True Faith in God)

20. Didascalia

21. Gregory Thaumaturgus—Discourse of Thanksgiving to Origen, Formula of Faith, Letter to the Bishops of Pontus, On the Passibility and Impassibility of God

22. Methodius—The Symposium [on Virginity],

23. Tertullian—To the Pagans (Ad Nationes), Apology, On the Testimony of the Soul, To Scapula, Against the Jews, De Praescriptione Haereticorum, Against Marcion, Against Hermogenes, Against Valentinian, On Baptism, Scorpiace, On the Body of Christ, On the Resurrection of the Flesh, Against Praxeas, On the Soul, On Prayer, On Penance, On Chastity, On the Dress of Women, On the Virgin's Veil, To His Wife, Exhortation to Chastity, On Monogamy, To the Martyrs, On Patience, De Spectaculis, On the Chaplet, Flight in Time of Persecution, Idolatry, De Pallio

24. Cyprian—82 Letters, To Donatus, To Demetrius, The Idols are not Gods, Testimonia Ad Quirinum, To Fortunatus (On Martyrdom), The Lapsed, The Unity of the Catholic Church, Mortality, On Prayer, The Good of Patience, The Dress of Virgins, Works and Almsgiving, Jealousy and Envy

25. Commodianus—Instructions, Carmen Apology

26. Arnobius—Against the Pagans

27. Lactantius—Divine Institutions

28. Hippolytus—Apostolic Tradition, Philosophoumena (Against All Heresies)

29. Herbert Musurillo's *Acts of the Christian Martyrs*

APPENDIX B

A Lexicon of Esteem

	HUMAN PORTRAYALS	SPIRITUAL PORTRAYALS
Native Americans	"The Indian lives now ... one of the great races." *(Indian Commissioner John Collier, 1942)*	"[Indians are] intelligent creatures of God." *(Bishop Henry Benjamin Whipple, 1859)*
African Americans	"The Negro was too much of a man to be held a chattel." *(Former slave Frederick Douglass, 1847)*	"God ... gave them [Africans] life and freedom." *(Petition to New Hampshire legislature, 1779)*
Soviet People	"They [kulaks] are human beings!" *(Former persecutor of kulaks, 1972)*	"[Gulag prisoners are] wise spiritual beings." *(Author Aleksandr Solzhenitsyn, 1973)*
European Jews	"Jews are men and women ... members of the human race." *(Archbishop Jules-Gerard Saliege's pastoral condemning Nazi persecution)*	"In this household, God's people are always welcome." *(Motivation of Ten Boom family for hiding Jews in Nazi-occupied Holland)*
Women	"[Women are] human beings ... human fellow-creatures." *(Philosopher John Stuart Mill, 1869)*	"Women [are] in Creation, noble ... in use, most blessed." *(Esther Soueman, 1617)*
Unborn Humans	"I will maintain the utmost respect for human life from the time of its conception." *(Declaration of Geneva World Medical Assn., 1948)*	"That unborn child has been carved in the hand of God." *(Nobel Prize speech of Mother Teresa, 1979)*
Dependent and/or Disabled Persons	"A human being who is deserving of food and water as you and I." *(Nurse Jeryl Turco s appeal for patient whose feeding tube was removed, 1987)*	"Immortal beings, children of one Father and heirs with Christ of eternal light." *(Mary Carpenter's defense of poor and neglected children, 1861)*

This chart is used by permission of the author and publisher, and can be found along with supporting documentation in: William Brennan, *Dehumanizing the Vulnerable: When Word Games Take Lives* (Lewiston, NY: Life Cycle, 1995) 21.

Appendix C

The Semantics of Oppression

Dehumanizing Terminology

B ECAUSE OF OUR NATURAL inclination against killing a fellow human being, the first step in the justification of violence is the act of
robbing the intended victim of his or her full humanity. This first step
is accomplished cognitively through the employment of dehumanizing
terminology, words chosen inadvertently or deliberately to depersonalize
the intended victim. By psychologically taking the proposed victim out
of the realm of human person, thereby distancing ourselves from those
whom we wish to make the objects of our violence, we can bypass our
moral reasoning which would normally cause us to hesitate before harming someone who we might otherwise think is like us. The astute observer
will discern the use of such dehumanizing rhetoric anywhere that an individual or group is marginalized or victimized.

William Brennan has documented the use of eight distinct categories of dehumanizing rhetoric used to make the act of harming or domi-
nating another human being more psychologically palatable by those
who would oppress, subjugate, or kill. The following chart, taken from his
Dehumanizing the Vulnerable: When Word Games Take Lives (Chicago:
Loyola University Press; Lewiston, NY: Life Cycle Books, 1995) and used
by gracious permission of the publisher, shows these eight categories
of dehumanizing rhetoric employed throughout history by those who
sought to justify the oppression or killing of various groups of vulnerable
victims. These groups of historically and currently oppressed peoples,
including Native Americans, African Americans, enemies of the former
Soviet Union, European Jews, women, unwanted unborn human life, and
the disabled, have little in common except for their status as victims of the
dehumanizing cycle that often leads to violence.

Notice the parallelism that occurs in the way that the victimizers refer to their intended victims across the centuries. The genocide of Native
Americans and the enslavement and oppression of African-Americans,
the murder of the European Jews, the Holocaust and extermination of

Soviet enemies, the oppression of women, and the disposal of unwanted unborn human life and the disabled and other "defective" human persons are all precipitated by the use of dehumanizing rhetoric that bypasses the human inclination against killing and justifies the oppression in the mind of the oppressor. The lesson for those of us committed to fighting violence and oppression, then, is to challenge and resist this rhetoric when we encounter it, but also to carefully police *ourselves*, our attitudes, and our own use of language so that we do not become victimizers ourselves.

DEHUMANIZING TERMINOLOGY

		DEFICIENT HUMAN	NONHUMAN	ANIMAL	PARASITE
VULNERABLE VICTIMS	Native Americans	"Indians [are] ... inferior to the Anglo-Saxon." *(Henry Clay, Sec. of State, 1825)*	"The life of these [aborigines] is ... not human." *(Author Hugh Brackenridge, 1779)*	"The Indian ... is an untamable, carnivorous animal." *(Dr. Josiah Noll, 1847)*	"Clear the country of that vermin [Indians]." *(Colonel Henry Bouquet, 1763)*
	African Americans	"A subordinate and inferior class of beings." *(U.S. Supreme Court on the status of Black people, 1857)*	"The negro is not a human being." *(Buckner Payne, Publisher, 1867)*	"The negro is ... one of the lower animals." *(Professor Charles Carroll, 1900)*	"They [Negroes] are parasites." *(Dr. T. Brady, 1909)*
	Soviet Enemies	"The uncivilized, stupid, turgid people in the Russian villages." *(Author Maxim Gorky, 1922)*	"Kulaks are not human beings." *(Lenin and Stalin, 1918–34)*	"[Peasants are] beasts of burden." *(George Plekhanov, founder of Russian Marxism, 1823)*	"The kulak, the parasite." *(Lenin, 1918)*
	European Jews	The inferior Jewish race." *(Dr. Rudolph Ramm, Nazi medical educator, 1943)*	"Jews are undoubtedly a race, but not human." *(Adolf Hitler, 1923)*	"The prisoners here are animals." *(Nazi anatomy prof. Dr. August Hirt, 1942)*	"The Jew is a parasite." *(Nazi propaganda booklet, 1944)*
	Women	"They [women] form ... the second sex, inferior in every respect to the first." *(Philosopher Arthur Schopenhauer, 1851)*	"Women are not seen as human." *(Report by women's group on pornographic images, 1980)*	"Women are domestic animals." *(19th-century poet Charles Baudelaire)*	"Women's sexual parasitism is innate." *(Philosopher Rene Guyon, 1950)*
	Unwanted Unborn	"The fetus, at most, represents only the potentiality of life." *(U.S. Supreme Court decision, 1973)*	"A fetus is not a human being." *(Rabbi Wolfe Kelman, 1984)*	"Like ... a primitive animal that's poked with a stick." *(Dr. Hart Peterson on fetal movement 1985)*	"The fetus is a parasite." *(Professor Rosalind Pollack Petchesky, 1984)*
	Dependent Discards	"A life ... devoid of those qualities which give it human dignity." *(Assessment of child with disability, Dr. Harry Hartzell, 1978)*	"No newborn infant should be declared human until it has passed certain tests." *(Dr. Francis Crick, 1978)*	"Until a living being can take conscious management of life ... it remains an animal." *(Prof. George Mill, 1981)*	"That's a real parasite." *(Medical staff characterization of a debilitated patient, 1989)*

DISEASE	INANIMATE OBJECT	WASTE PRODUCT	NONPERSON
"The Iroquois had proved more deadly . . . than the pestilence." (Historian Francis Parkman, 1902)	"[Indians are] anthropological specimens." (American press coverage, 1904)	"[Indians are] the very dregs, garbage . . . of Earth." (Poet Christopher Brooke, 1622)	"An Indian is not a person within the meaning of the Constitution." (George Canfield, Am. Law Rev., 1881)
"Free black in our country are . . . a contagion." (American Colonization Soc., 1815-30)	"A negro of the African race was regarded . . . as an article of property." (U.S. Supreme Court decision, 1857)	"The negro race is . . . a heritage of organic and psychic debris." (Dr. William English, 1903)	"In the eyes of the law . . . the slave is not a person." (Virginia Supreme Court decision, 1858)
"Every religious idea [is] . . . 'contagion' of the most abominable kind." (Lenin, 1913)	"[Gulag slave laborers are] raw material." (Author Maxim Gorky, 1934)	"A foul-smelling heap of human garbage [Purge Trial Defendants]." (Prosecutor Andrei Vyshinsky, 1938)	"Unpersons who had never existed." (Designation for people purged by the Soviet government)
"Some day Europe will perish of the Jewish disease." (Joseph Goebbels, Nazi Propaganda Minister, 1939)	"Transit material." (Portrayal of Jews dispatched to Nazi death camps, 1942-44)	"What shall we do with this garbage [Jews]?" (Christian Wirth, extermination expert, 1942)	"The Reichsgericht itself refused to recognize Jews . . . as 'persons' in the legal sense." (1936 German Supreme Conti decision)
"The worst plague Zeus has made— women." (Ancient Greek poet Semonides)	"I considered my wife. my property." (Former wife abuser, 1989)	"Emptying refuse into a sewer [the woman's body]." (Author Henry Miller, /965)	"The Statutory word 'person' did not in these circumstances include women." (British voting rights case, 1909)
"Pregnancy when not wanted is a disease . . . in fact, a venereal disease." (Professor Joseph Fletcher, 1979)	"People's body parts [embryos] are their personal property " (Attorney Lori Andrews, 1986)	"An aborted baby is just garbage . . . Just refuse." (Dr. Martti Kekomaki, 1980)	"The word 'person,' as used in the 14th Amendment, does not include the unborn." (U.S. Supreme Court decision, 1973)
"Those 'sicklers.'" (Doctors' portrayal of patients with sickle cell anemia, 1986)	"I came to see the patients as work objects." (Nursing home staff member, 1977)	"There's a lot of rubbish [patients] this morning." (ER doctor, 1979)	"New-born humans are neither persons nor even quasi- persons." (Philosopher Michael Tooley, 1983)

Modern Sources Cited

Alan Guttmacher Institute, *Induced Abortion, Facts in Brief,* 2002. Online: http://www
.infoplease.com/ipa/A0904509.html.

Army of God. "Defensive Action Statement." Online: http://www.armyofgod.com/defense
.html.

———. "Second Defensive Action Statement." Online: http://www.armyofgod.com/
defense2.html.

Bogue, Edith. "Does the Seamless Garment Fit? American Public Opinion." In *Consistently
Opposing Killing: From Abortion to Assisted Suicide, the Death Penalty, and War,* edited
by Rachel M. MacNair and Stephen Zunes, 73–86. Westport, CN: Praeger, 2008.

Brennan, William. *Dehumanizing the Vulnerable: When Word Games Take Lives.* Chicago:
Loyola University Press, 1995.

Callahan, Sidney. "Abortion and the Sexual Agenda: A Case for Prolife Feminism."
In *Feminist Ethics and the Catholic Moral Tradition*, edited by Charles E. Curran,
Margaret A. Farley, and Richard A. McCormick, S.J., 422–39. Mahwah, NJ: Paulist,
1996.

Davey, Monica. "Closed Clinic Leaves Abortion Protesters at a Loss." *New York Times* (June
7, 2009). Online: http://www.nytimes.com/2009/06/08/us/08wichita.html.

Duin, Julia. "Doctor Likens Tiller's Killing to MLK's." *Washington Times* (June 9, 2009).
Online: http://washingtontimes.com/news/2009/jun/09/tiller-likened-to-mlk/.

———. "MLK Kin Decries Comparison to Tiller." *Washington Times* (June 10, 2009).
Online: http://www.washingtontimes.com/news/2009/jun/10/tiller-family-plans-to-
shutter-abortion-clinic/.

ELCA Social Statement on Abortion. Approved August 1991. Online: http://archive.elca.
org/socialstatements/abortion/.

Erdahl, Lowell O. *Pro-Life/Pro-Peace: Life-Affirming Alternatives to Abortion, War, Mercy
Killing, and the Death Penalty.* Minneapolis: Augsburg, 1986.

Fausset, Richard. "A History of Violence on the Antiabortion Fringe." *Los Angeles Times*
(June 1, 2009). Online: http://articles.latimes.com/2009/jun/01/nation/na-abortion-
violence1.

Goldman, John J. "Bomb Plot Architect Gets Life Term." *Los Angeles Times* (January 19,
1998). Online: http://articles.latimes.com/1998/jan/09/news/mn-6644.

Grossman, Dave, *On Killing: The Psychological Cost of Learning to Kill in War and Society.*
Boston: Little Brown, 1995.

Gudorf, Christine. "Heroes, Suicide, and Moral Discernment." *Journal of the Society of
Christian Ethics* 29 (2009) 87–108.

Hays, Richard B. *The Moral Vision of the New Testament: Community, Cross, New
Creation. A Contemporary Introduction to New Testament Ethics.* San Francisco:
HarperSanFrancisco, 1996.

Modern Sources Cited

Hauerwas, Stanley. "Abortion, Theologically Considered." In *Virtues and Practices in the Christian Tradition: Christian Ethics after MacIntyre,* edited by Nancey Murphy, Brad J. Kallenberg, and Mark Thiessen Nation, 221–38. Harrisburg, PA: Trinity, 1997.

————. "Sacrificing the Sacrifices of War." *Criswell Theological Review* 4 (2007) 77–95.

Hentoff, Nat. "The Indivisibility of Life and the Slippery Slope." In *Consistently Opposing Killing: From Abortion to Assisted Suicide, the Death Penalty, and War,* edited by Rachel M. MacNair and Stephen Zunes, 25–32. Westport, CN: Praeger, 2008.

Hill, Paul. "Should We Defend Born and Unborn Children with Force?" Online: http://www.mttu.com/Articles/Should%20We%20Defend%20Born%20And%20Unborn%20Children%20With%20Force.htm.

Kavanaugh, John F., S.J. *Who Counts as Persons? Human Identity and the Ethics of Killing.* Washington, DC: Georgetown University Press, 2001.

King, Martin Luther, Jr. "A Christmas Sermon on Peace." In *A Testament of Hope: The Essential Writings of Martin Luther King Jr.,* edited by James Melvin Washington, 253–58. San Francisco: Harper & Row, 1986.

————. "A Time to Break Silence." In *A Testimony of Hope: The Essential Writings of Martin Luther King Jr.,* edited by James Melvin Washington, 231–52. San Francisco: Harper & Row, 1986.

Kyle, Donald G. *Spectacles of Death in Ancient Rome.* New York: Routledge, 1998.

Marshall, S. L. A. *Men Against Fire: The Problem of Battle Command.* Norman: University of Oklahoma Press, 2000.

Mason, Carol. *Killing For Life: The Apocalyptic Narrative of Pro-Life Violence.* Ithaca, NY: Cornell University Press, 2002.

McVeigh, Timothy. "An Essay on Hypocrisy." *Media Bypass* (June, 1998). Online: http://linkage.rockefeller.edu/wli/reading/mcv.html.

Meehan, Mary. "The Left Has Betrayed the Sanctity of Life: Consistency Demands Concern for the Unborn." In *Consistently Opposing Killing: From Abortion to Assisted Suicide, the Death Penalty, and War,* edited by Rachel M. MacNair and Stephen Zunes, 19–24. Westport, CN: Praeger, 2008.

Morrison, Clinton. *The Powers That Be: Earthly Rulers and Demonic Powers in Romans 13:1–7.* London: SCM, 1960.

Murch Bruce Evan. "Eulogy for Paul Hill." Http://www.covenantnews.com/murch030905.htm.

Newman, Troy. Statement on Operation Rescue's website (June 9, 2009). Online: http://www.operationrescue.org/archives/tiller-clinic-will-permanently-close-while-ksbha-says-abortion-investigation-still-pending/. (Accessed June 15, 2009).

Peikoff, Leonard. "Abortion Rights are Pro-Life." Online: http://www.abortionisprolife.com/abortion-rights-are-pro-life.htm.

Reno, R. R. "Defending Life Requires Law." *On the Square* blog (June 3, 2009). Online: http://www.firstthings.com/on_the_square_entry.php?year=2009&month=6&title_link=defending-life-requires-law.

Rice, Charles. "Can the Killing of Abortionists Be Justified?" *The Wanderer* (September 1, 1994). Online: http://www.ewtn.com/library/PROLIFE/KILLJUST.TXT.

Rucker, Phillip. "Pro-Life Activist Says Doctor 'Reaped What He Sowed.'" *Washington Post* (June 1, 2009). Online: http://www.washingtonpost.com/wp-dyn/content/article/2009/06/01/AR2009060102058.html. (Accessed June 12, 2009).

Scalia, Elizabeth. "Tiller, Long, Bonhoeffer, and Assassination." *On the Square* blog (June 4, 2009). Online: http://www.firstthings.com/on_the_square_entry.php?year=2009 &month=6&title_link=tiller-long-bonhoeffer-and-ass.

Shields Jon A. "A Time To Kill: Why Is Anti-Abortion Violence at an All-Time High When Radical Pro-Life Activism Is on the Decline?" *The New Republic* (June 2, 2009). Online: http://www.tnr.com/politics/story.html?id=409ed7ae-76fa-411c-9720-6182 15852f11.

Siemon-Netto, Uwe. "Remembering Collective Shame." Online blog: http://concordia .typepad.com/vocation/2008/10/remembering-col.html.

Stark, Rodney. *The Rise of Christianity: How the Obscure, Marginal Jesus Movement Became the Dominant Religious Force in the Western World in a Few Centuries.* Princeton, NJ: Princeton University Press, 1996.

Steiner, Mark Allan. *The Rhetoric of Operation Rescue: Projecting the Christian Pro-Life Message.* New York: T. & T. Clark, 2006.

Veazey, Carlton W. On behalf of the Religious Coalition for Reproductive Choice (June 1, 2009). Online: http://www.rcrc.org/news/Dr%20Tiller_1.cfm.

Warner, Judith. "Dr. Tiller's Important Job." *New York Times* (June 4, 2009). Online: http:// warner.blogs.nytimes.com/2009/06/04/george-tiller/.

Waskow, Arthur. "Murder is Murder and Abortion is Not." *Washington Post.* Online: http://newsweek.washingtonpost.com/onfaith/panelists/arthur_waskow/2009/06/ murder_is_murder_abortion_is_not.html.

Wright, N. T. "Romans." In *The New Interpreter's Bible*, vol. 10. Nashville: Abingdon, 1994.

Yoder, John Howard. *The Politics of Jesus: Vicit Agnus Noiter.* 2nd ed. Grand Rapids: Eerdmans 1994.

———. *The Priestly Kingdom: Social Ethics as Gospel.* Notre Dame, IN: University of Notre Dame Press, 1984.

Young, Curt. *The Least of These.* Chicago: Moody, 1983.

Works Cited by or about Ancient Christians

This list of sources represents only the volumes that are explicitly cited or mentioned in this book. For readers without access to theological libraries who wish to access the ancient Christian writers to read further, most of the patristic sources can be found at http://www.ccel.org. Alternatively, patristic sources up to and including Origen can be accessed at http://www.earlychristianwritings.com. The translations available online are much older than the volumes I consulted, however, so they may be difficult to read at some points and will not necessarily match up with the translations as I've cited them in this book.

Aristides. *The Apology of Aristides*. Online: http://www.earlychristianwritings.com/text/aristides-kay.html.

Arnobius, and George Englert McCracken. *The Case against the Pagans*, Ancient Christian Writers; No. 7–8. Westminster, MD: Newman, 1949.

Athenagoras. *Embassy for the Christians. The Resurrection of the Dead*. Translated by Joseph Hugh Crehan. Ancient Christian Writers 23. Westminster, MD: Newman, 1956.

Bainton, Roland Herbert. *Christian Attitudes toward War and Peace: A Historical Survey and Critical Re-Evaluation*. New York: Abingdon, 1960.

———. "The Early Church and War." *Harvard Theological Review* 93 (1946) 189–212.

Brock, Peter. *The Military Question in the Early Church: A Selected Bibliography of a Century's Scholarship, 1888–1987*. Toronto: Self-Published, 1988.

Cadoux, Cecil John. *The Early Christian Attitude to War: A Contribution to the History of Christian Ethics*. The Christian Revolution Series 8. London: Headley, 1919.

Clement, and John Ferguson. *Stromateis: Books 1–3*. Translated by John Ferguson. The Fathers of the Church 23. Washington, DC: Catholic University of America Press, 1991.

Clement of Alexandria. *Christ the Educator*. Translated by Simon P. Wood, vol. 23: *The Fathers of the Church*. Washington, DC: The Catholic University of America Press, 1954.

———. *Clement of Alexandria*. Translated by G. W. Butterworth. Cambridge: Harvard University Press, 1982.

Clement of Rome, and Ignatius of Antioch. *The Epistles of St. Clement of Rome and St. Ignatius of Antioch*. Translated by James Aloysious Kleist. Ancient Christian Writers 1. Westminster, MD: Newman, 1946.

Cyprian. *Saint Cyprian: Treatises*. Translated by Roy J. Deferrari. The Fathers of the Church 36. New York: Fathers of the Church, 1958.

Cyprian, and Maurice Bévenot. *The Lapsed, and The Unity of the Catholic Church*. Ancient Christian Writers 25. Westminster, MD: Newman, 1957.

Works Cited by or about Ancient Christians

Cyprian, and G. W. Clarke. *The Letters of St. Cyprian of Carthage*. 4 vols. Ancient Christian Writers 43–44, 46–47. New York: Paulist, 1984.

Gorman, Michael J. *Abortion & the Early Church: Christian, Jewish & Pagan Attitudes in the Greco-Roman World*. Downers Grove, IL: InterVarsity, 1982.

Harnack, Adolf von. *Militia Christi: The Christian Religion and the Military in the First Three Centuries*. Philadelphia: Fortress, 1981.

Helgeland, John. "Christians and the Roman Army Ad 173–337." *Church History* 43 (1974) 149–63.

———. "Civil Religion, Military Religion: Roman and American." *Forum* (1989) 22–44.

———. "The Early Church and War: The Sociology of Idolatry." In *Peace in a Nuclear Age*, edited by Charles J Reid, 34–47. Washington, DC: Catholic University of America Press, 1986.

Helgeland, John, Robert J. Daly, and J. Patout Burns. *Christians and the Military: The Early Experience*. Philadelphia: Fortress, 1985.

Hippolytus. *On the Apostolic Tradition*. Translated by Alistair Stewart-Sykes. St. Vladimir's Seminary Press "Popular Patristics." Crestwood, NY: St. Vladimir's Seminary Press, 2001.

Hornus, Jean Michel. *It Is Not Lawful for Me to Fight: Early Christian Attitudes toward War, Violence, and the State*. Rev. ed. Scottdale, PA: Herald, 1980.

Irenaeus. *Proof of the Apostolic Preaching*. Translated by Joseph P. Smith. Ancient Christian Writers 16. Westminster, MD: Newman, 1952.

Irenaeus, Dominic J. Unger, and John J. Dillon. *Against the Heresies*. Ancient Christian Writers 55. New York: Paulist, 1992.

Justin Martyr. *The Dialogue with Trypho*. Translated by A. Lukyn Williams. London: SPCK, 1930.

———. *The First and Second Apologies*. Translated by Leslie W. Barnard. Ancient Christian Writers 56. New York: Paulist, 1997.

Kyle, Donald G. *Spectacles of Death in Ancient Rome*. New York: Routledge, 1998.

Lactantius. *The Divine Institutes, Books I-VII*. Translated by Mary Francis McDonald. The Fathers of the Church 49. Washington: Catholic University of America Press, 1964.

Lohfink, Gerhard. *Jesus and Community: The Social Dimension of Christian Faith*. Translated by John P. Galvin. Philadelphia: Fortress, 1984.

Minucius Felix, Marcus, and G. W. Clarke. *The Octavius of Marcus Minucius Felix*. Ancient Christian Writers 39. New York: Newman, 1974.

Musurillo, Herbert. *The Acts of the Christian Martyrs*. Oxford Early Christian Texts. Oxford: Clarendon, 1972.

Novatian. *The Trinity, The Spectacles, Jewish Foods, In Praise of Purity, Letters*. Translated by Russell J. DeSimone. The Fathers of the Church 67. Washington, DC: Catholic University of America Press, 1972.

Origen. *Contra Celsum*. Translated by Henry Chadwick. Cambridge: Cambridge University Press, 1980.

Origen, and John Joseph O'Meara. *Prayer* and *Exhortation to Martyrdom*. Ancient Christian Writers 19. Westminster, MD: Newman, 1954.

Polycarp, and Papias. *The Didache. The Epistle of Barnabas. The Epistles and the Martyrdom of St. Polycarp. The Fragments of Papias. The Epistle to Diognetus*. Translated by James Aloysius Kleist. Ancient Christian Writers 6. Westminster, MD: Newman, 1948.

Richardson, Cyril Charles. *Early Christian Fathers*. The Library of Christian Classics 1. New York: Macmillan, 1970.

Roberts, Alexander, James Donaldson, A. Cleveland Coxe, Allan Menzies, Ernest Cushing Richardson, and Bernhard Pick. *The Ante-Nicene Fathers: Translations of the Writings of the Fathers Down to A.D. 325*. 10 vols. Grand Rapids: Eerdmanns, 1986.

Ronsse, Erin. "Rhetoric of Martyrs: Listening to Saints Perpetua and Felicitas." *Journal of Early Christian Studies* 14 (2006) 283–327.

Salisbury, Joyce E. *The Blood of Martyrs: Unintended Consequences of Ancient Violence*. New York: Routledge, 2004.

Swift, Louis J. *The Early Fathers on War and Military Service*. Message of the Fathers of the Church 19. Wilmington, DE: Glazier, 1983.

Tatian. *Oratio ad Graecos and Fragments*. Translated by Molly Whittaker. Oxford Early Christian Texts. Oxford New York: Clarendon, 1982.

Tertullian. *Adversus Marcionem*. Translated by Ernest Evans. Oxford: Clarendon, 1972.

———. *Tertullian: Disciplinary, Moral, and Ascetical Works*. Translated by Sister Emily Joseph Daly Rudolph Arbesmann, Edwin A. Quain. The Fathers of the Church 40. New York: Fathers of the Church, 1959.

———. *Treatises on Penance: On Penitence and On Purity*. Translated by William P. Le Saint. Ancient Christian Writers 28. Westminster, MD: Newman, 1959.

Tertullian, Jan Hendrik Waszink, J. C. M. van Winden, and P. G. van der Nat. *De Idololatria: Critical Text, Translation, and Commentary*. Supplements to Vigiliae Christianae 1. Leiden: Brill, 1987.

Tertullian. *Apologetical Works, and Minicius Felix: Octavius*. Translated by Rudolph Arbesmann, Sister Emily Joseph Daly, and Edwin A. Quain. The Fathers of the Church 10. New York: Fathers of the Church, Inc., 1950.

Webster, Alexander F. C. *The Pacifist Option: The Moral Argument against War in Eastern Orthodox Moral Theology*. San Francisco: International Scholars, 1998.

Wengst, Klaus. *Pax Romana and the Peace of Jesus Christ*. Translated by John Bowden. Philadelphia: Fortress, 1987.